STEPHEN BAR SUDAILI

THE SYRIAN MYSTIC

AND

THE BOOK OF HIEROTHEOS.

STEPHEN BAR SUDAILI

THE SYRIAN MYSTIC

AND

THE BOOK OF HIEROTHEOS.

BY

A. L. FROTHINGHAM. Jr.

WIPF & STOCK · Eugene, Oregon

Wipf and Stock Publishers
199 W 8th Ave, Suite 3
Eugene, OR 97401

Stephen bar Sudaili, The Syrian Mystic and The Book of Hierotheos
By Frothingham, Arthur Lincoln
ISBN 13: 978-1-60899-607-0
Publication date 4/5/2010
Previously published by Brill, 1886

TABLE OF CONTENTS.

Introduction: the mystico-pantheistic schools of Egypt and Syria . . . . p. 1.

Ch. I. The writings of Pseudo-Dionysios; their spread in Syria, and long-continued influence through the Middle-Ages . . . . „ 2.

Ch. II. Stephen Bar Sudaili, the East-Syrian mystic. Was he the author of the Book of Hierotheos and the master of Pseudo-Dionysios? . . . . „ 6.

Ch. III. Letter of Jacob of Sarug to Stephen Bar Sudaili, supporting against him the Church doctrine of the eternity of punishment. Syriac text and translation „ 11.

Ch. IV. Letter of Philoxenos or Xenaias of Mabûg to Stephen and Orestes concerning Bar Sudaili; exposing his pantheistic doctrine of the consubstantiality of God and the material Universe, and the redemption of all existence by assimilation to the divine principle. Syriac text and translation . . . . „ 20.

Ch. V. The philosophic system of Bar Sudaili, as expounded in the preceding letters, compared with the Book of Hierotheos and the Dionysian fragments of Hierotheos . . . . „ 49.

Ch. VI. Biography of Bar Sudaili. His birth at Edessa. Probability of his temporary residence in Egypt: documents confirming this hypothesis. His return to Edessa and subsequent residence in or near Jerusalem, shortly after A. D. 500 . . . . „ 56.

Ch. VII. Bar Sudaili considered by Syrian writers, — e. g. Kyriakos of Antioch, John of Dara, and Gregory Bar ᶜEbraia, — to be the author of the Book of Hierotheos . . . . p. 63.

Ch. VIII. The Book of Hierotheos preserved in a Syriac MS. of the British Museum. Is this Syriac text the original, or a version from a lost Greek original? Reasons for considering the assertion of a Greek original to be a part of the fraud . . . . „ 69.

Ch. IX. The high position given by Pseudo-Dionysios to his master Hierotheos. He claims only to expand and present to the uninitiated the ideas of his master. A comparison of the two writers . . . . „ 74.

Ch. X. The question of priority: was the Book of Hierotheos produced in view of the Dionysian writings, or was it an original and anterior production? . . . „ 81.

Ch. XI. The commentaries of Theodosios of Antioch and Gregory Bar ᶜEbraia on the Book of Hierotheos . . . „ 84.

Ch. XII. Summary of the «Book of Hierotheos on the Hidden Mysteries of the Divinity» . . . . „ 91.

Book I. On the Good, the Universal Essence, and distinct existences . . . . „ 92.

Book II. The various species of motion: the ascent of the mind towards the Good, during which it must endure the sufferings of Christ . . . „ 96.

Book III. The resurrection of the mind, the vicissitudes of its conflict with the powers of evil, and its final identification with Christ . . . „ 100.

Book IV. The mind becomes one, first with Christ, then with the Spirit and the Father, and finally becomes absorbed . . . . „ 102.

Book V. All nature becomes confounded with the Father; all distinct existence and God himself passes away; Essence alone remains . . . . „ 110.

During the first centuries of Christianity, East Syria and Egypt were the two great centres of false mysticism and pantheism, and between them there ever existed the closest relations. Although Egyptian thought and the Valentinian system exercised a great influence over Syrian thought, yet the latter possessed certain special characteristics; for while the Alexandrian schools threw their universal eclecticism into the mould of Greek thought, and gave a philosophical character to their speculations, the Syrian schools were distinguished by a vivid fancy and a bold speculation, to which they did not seek to give a philosophical or a logical form. On the other hand, if we try to connect by analogy the Syrian Gnostics and mystics with preceding systems of thought, we easily perceive the close relation in which they stood to the later Persian system, to the debased Chaldaean worship, and to the Jewish Kabbala, which probably flourished in their very midst among the Jewish settlements of Babylonia.

The doctrines of Bardesanes and of Manes preserved great force and influence in the East Syrian Church, even until the middle of the fourth century, when S. Ephraem wrote and labored against them with all the influence he could wield, as heresies which had deep root among all classes. From this time forward Syrian mysticism took a more ecclesiastical form, and pantheistic doctrine became subtly infused into the orthodox forms of belief, producing a steadily progressive inversion of the Christian faith.

I. THE WRITINGS OF PSEUDO-DIONYSIOS.

After the epoch of S. Ephraem († 373) we do not hear of any prominent movement in the mystical school of Syria until the last years of the fifth century or the first of the succeeding, when there suddenly appeared a body of writings purporting to be by Dionysios the Areopagite, the convert of Saint Paul [1]). It has been for some time generally recognized that they were the work of this period [2]), and, in all probability, written by some follower of Proclus [3]), who may have been a Syrian monk [4]); a theory supported by the fact that, although eagerly received and studied by the whole East, these writings were brought forward and most powerfully supported by the Syrians. All mystics recognized these works to be the production of a master-mind, worthy of becoming their guide in pantheistic speculation. The extent to which they were used can be appreciated on consulting Syriac mss., where Dionysios is adduced as authority in most controversial writings, especially by the Monophysites.

But it was not only the mystical schools and the Eastern

1) S. Dionysii Areopagitae Opera omnia stud. et op. Balth. Corderii: Migne, Patr. Graecae T. III and IV. Darboy (l'abbé), Œuvres de Saint Denis l'Aréopagite. Paris 1845.

Cf. J. Dulac, Œuvres de Saint Denis l'Aréopagite. Paris 1865.

2) Gieseler, A text-book of Church history, New-York 1857, vol. I, p. 468. Schaff, History of the Christian Church, vol. III, p. 604. Baur, Geschichte der Kirche, T. II, p. 59—65. Gfrörer, Allgemeine Kirchengeschichte, 1840. II Buch. p. 902. Dorner, Doctrine of the person of Christ: Div. II, vol. I, p. 157 and 422. etc. etc.

3) Engelhardt, Baur, Gfrörer, Schaff, etc. Dorner connects him with the Monophysites.

4) Gfrörer, ibid. p. 912. Gieseler, ibid. considers him to have flourished in Egypt and to coincide with Cyrill in the doctrine of the person of Christ!! Westcott (Contemp. Review, May 1867) thinks that the Pseudo-Dionysian writings «were composed A.D. 480—520, either at Edessa or under the influence of the Edessa School". This judgment is founded on the relation to Bar Sudaili.

heretics that supported the Pseudo-Dionysian writings. The orthodox at first protested against them at the Council of Constantinople in 533, and denied their genuineness, by the mouth of Hypatius, who attributed them to the Apollinarists; but it was not long before they accepted them as genuine, for, besides an affinity for such speculation being wide-spread at this time, they could find in these works many arguments and proofs in favor of Church institutions and ecclesiastical authority; and from these two causes the Pseudo-Dionysian writings were accepted even by the Popes, as by Gregory the Great [1]), Martin I [2]), and Agatho [3]).

Almost contemporaneously with the appearance of the Dionysian writings there appeared also a Syriac version of them, rendered necessary by the favor they were obtaining throughout Syria. The author of this version was Sergius the archiater or physician of Ras'ain († 536), the famous Aristotelian and writer on medicine [4]). It is a characteristic phenomenon that a follower of Aristotle should find the greatest of false mystics a congenial spirit, and should become thoroughly impregnated with his doctrines: that it was so with Sergius is shown even more clearly by the long introduction which he prefixed to his version of the Pseudo-Dionysios [5]), where he shows himself to be not a simple translator but an original thinker in mysticism. Of course the Alexandrian school was the link between the two. In this connection it is interesting to note a passage in a contemporary work, the ecclesiastical history attributed to Zacharias Rhetor, in which Sergius is characterized as an eloquent man and learned »in

1) In his 34th homily, on the Gospel of S. Luke, ch. 15.
2) Acta Synodi Lateran. a. 660.
3) Letter to the Emp. Constantine for the Council of Constantinople, a. 680.
4) This version is contained in Brit. Mus. Add. 12.151 and 12.152, etc.
5) Brit. Mus. Add. 22.370.

Greek literature and in the *doctrine of Origen*" [1]. The Origenistic revival of the beginning of the sixth century was in perfect accord with the theories of the Pseudo-Dionysios; still it is interesting to note this further connection.

The writers who have undertaken to trace the development of the influence of the Pseudo-Areopagite have confined themselves to Greek and Latin literature, and have neglected the very important part taken by Syrian writers in this movement. It was in reality as important as either of the former, and can boast nearly as many noteworthy representatives. Contemporary with the scholia of John of Scythopolis, for example, who was the first Greek commentator of Dionysios, we find the version and scholia of Sergius of Ras'ain, already mentioned; and while the next Greek commentator is the noted Maximus, who flourished in the seventh century, Syria is represented again in the sixth century itself by the monk Joseph Huzaja, who wrote a ܦܘܫܩ ܕܝܘܢܘܣܝܘܣ "Commentary on Dionysios" [2]. Afterwards, and not quite a century later than Maximus, appear the commentaries of Phocas bar Sergius of Edessa [3] and John bishop of Dara [4]. This latter treats only of the Celestial and Ecclesiastical Hierarchies and does not confine itself to the office of a commentary, but holds forth original views in various chapters. During the latest period of Syriac literature we find the commentary of Theodore bar Zarudi of Edessa [5]. It would not be possible in the present incomplete state of our acquaintance with Syrian literature to give a satisfactory account

---

1) Land, Anecdota Syriaca T. III, p. 289.

2) 'Ebed Yeshu, Catal. of Syrian writers, in Assem. Bib. Or. T. III, P. I, p. 103.

3) W. Wright, Catal. of the Syriac mss. of the Brit. Mus. T. II, p. 493. The MS. is dated A.D. 804.

4) Assemani Catal. Codd. Syr. T. II, p. 530: cf. Bib. Or. T. II, p. 120.

5) W. Wright, op. cit., p. 500. MS. Add 22.370, of the XIV or XV century.

of the early Syrian writers who have mentioned Dionysios or followed his doctrines. Still we can mention during the sixth century such distinguished men as Severus of Antioch, Isaac of Nineveh [1]), John of Apamea [2]) and Peter of Callinicus, Patriarch of Antioch [3]).

At the time when, with the opening of a new period in the ninth century, religious thought took a new form and scholastic theology began its rule, the influence of the Pseudo-Dionysios increased rather than waned, and it continued throughout the constructive period of Scholasticism. He was made the authority, the starting-point, of most of the theories put forth, in one form by the founder of Scholasticism John Erigena, and in others by the school of St. Victor, by the German mystics Eckhart and Tauler, and by Thomas Aquinas himself. A writer has remarked that, if the writings of Dionysios had been lost, they could be almost reconstituted from the works of Aquinas [4]). To read Buonaventura, especially his tract "Itinerarium mentis in Deum", carries one back to Dionysios as his immediate inspiring source.

Now Pseudo-Dionysios confesses to having had two teachers in the faith, S. Paul and one named Hierotheos [5]); the for-

---

1) Besides his mention of Dionysios' Celest. Hierarchy (cf. Assem. B. O. I, 451) in his sermon "De materia quam exigit anima ut a corporeis cogitationibus etc.", there are indications that Isaac was himself a mystical writer. 'Ebed Yeshu in his catal. gives the titles of two of his writings which were evidently of this character: 1) ܥܠ ܕܘܒܪܐ ܕܪܘܚܐ "on the government of the spirit", and 2) ܥܠ ܐܪ̈ܙܐ ܐܠܗ̈ܝܐ "on the Divine mysteries".

2) See in Cod. Syr. Vat. XCIII his treatises and letters: 1) on spiritual government; 2) on the incomprehensibility of God; 3) on spiritual communion with God.

3) He quotes Dionysios (Div. Names ch. I and V) in his Libri contra Damianum L. II, ch. 41 and 47; see Cod. Syr. Vat. CVIII f. 282 sqq.

4) J. Dulac, Oeuvres de S. Denys l'Aréopagite, traduites du grec, p. 105.

5) Divine Names II, 11.

mer is of course a fiction, the latter may have more reality. Hierotheos is praised by him in the most glowing terms, as divine, as an inspired mystic, whose writings are a second Bible, *δεύτερα λόγια* [1]), and whose knowledge of divine things was far above his own. The fragments of his writings given by Pseudo-Dionysios are interesting: they are taken from his *Ἐρωτικοὶ ὕμνοι*, *Erotic Hymns* [2]), and from a work entitled *Θεολογικαὶ στοιχειώσεις*, *The Elements of Theology* [3]). If, as is well known, the whole of scholastic theology and of mediaeval mysticism is founded on the doctrines of the Pseudo-Dionysios, of what extraordinary interest would it not be to discover the very source of these doctrines, their origin in a form more abstract than that given by the Pseudo-Areopagite! Hence it was often asked by the followers of the latter: who was this Hierotheos? what were his writings? what is known of him? These questions remained unanswered, for nothing could be gleaned concerning such a man except from the Dionysian writings themselves. Then the question naturally followed: did such a person ever exist? was he not a mere Dionysian figment? [4]).

We hope to give in tho following pages an answer to some of these questions, and will present in outline an unpublished work, hitherto unknown to students of this subject, claiming to be written by Hierotheos, and which may or may not be really by the master of the Pseudo-Dionysios.

II. STEPHEN BAR SUDAILI.

To the very period now almost unanimously assigned to

---

1) Div. Names, ch. III, § II.
2) Div. Names, ch. IV, § XV, XVI, and XVII.
3) Div. Names, ch. II, § X, and probably Eccl. Hier. ch. II, p. 1.
4) Dallaeus, *Pseudo-Dionysius Areopagita.*

the production of the Pseudo-Dionysiana belongs a prominent and interesting figure in the Syrian Church, that of the mystic Stephen Bar Sudaili. The connection of these two phenomena is not by any means fortuitous, but the materials available up to the present have been so few that his position and individuality have never been clearly defined [1]).

Among the letters of Philoxenos of Mabûg is one written to Abraham and Orestes, priests of Edessa, concerning Bar Sudaili [2]): this document is the principal source from which we derive our information regarding him, for the letter of Jacob of Sarug addressed to Bar Sudaili himself adds but little [3]), and the few other notices we have been able to collect referring to the latter do so in but few words.

Bar Sudaili is important, not only as a prominent representative of the mystical school of East Syria, but as being connected with an interesting literary and religious question, the solution of which has never been attempted: that is, whether or no he is the author of the Book of Hierotheos, and in what relation this work stands to the writings of the Pseudo-Dionysios, who asserts Hierotheos to have been his master [4]). To collect and present all the available material relating to this subject is what I will attempt to accomplish in a short while, so that competent judges may have the opportunity of forming their opinion on the question. In order to do this I hope to publish before long the complete

1) Asseman being the common source of all that has been said on Bar Sudaili, the only difference is in the variety of construction placed upon his words.

2) See page 28.

3) See page 10.

4) The probable identity of Bar Sudaili and Pseudo-Hierotheos has been assumed, on the sole authority of Bar 'Ebraia, e. g. by Zöckler in his article on B. S. in Herzog's Real Encyk. (T. XV. p. 203—5), who is followed in the Cyclop. of Messrs Clintock and Strong (vol. X, p. 8—9).

text of the Book of Hierotheos in the so-called Syriac version of a supposed Greek original now lost. The unique copy of this version has long lain unnoticed among the treasures of the British Museum. For the present I will limit myself to giving, in this essay, the letters of Philoxenos and Jacob of Sarug with a translation, and an abstract of the Book of Hierotheos, together with a few extracts which will illustrate its principles and the form of its thought and language. As a necessary introduction to this analysis will be given, as far as is possible, the chain of judgments on and references to the Book of Hierotheos which are found among Syrian writers.

The conditions necessary to the formation of a judgment, from the intrinsic evidence, on the probability of Bar Sudaili being the author are, after examining the analysis and refutation of the doctrines of Bar Sudaili in the letters of Philoxenos and Jacob of Sarug, in the first place, to compare these doctrines with those of the Book of Hierotheos, and, in the second place, to decide whether there is a perfect correspondence between the latter and the fragments of the "Elements of Theology" and the "Erotic Hymns" of Hierotheos quoted by the Pseudo-Dionysios in his book on the "Divine Names" and in his "Eccles. Hierarchy". Finally we must see whether there are any other documents which connect Bar Sudaili with the supposed Hierotheos.

The two letters concerning Bar Sudaili have been known principally through the full analysis of that of Philoxenos given by Asseman in his "Bibliotheca Orientalis" [1]); and many church

1) T. II, p. 30 sqq.; cf. T. I, p. 303.

historians, such as Neander[1]), Gfrörer[2]), Dorner[3]), etc., have, on the strength of this, assigned to Bar Sudaili an important position, as illustrating the mystical side of Monophysitism and the influence of the Origenistic revival. His pantheism, which is fully recognized by them, can now be made to appear in a still clearer light by the publication of the texts themselves. The letter of Philoxenos bishop of Hierapolis is written in an exquisitely pure Syriac, and will be all the more welcome that the writings of this purest of Syriac writers, though very extensive, have been entirely neglected and remain inedited. The letter of Jacob of Sarug, though it does not furnish many additional data, and does not show much theological acuteness, is a good specimen of his flowery diction and persuasive language.

---

1) General History of the Christian Religion and Church, v. II, p. 555—557.
2) Allgemeine Kirchengeschichte, 1840, T. II, p. 902.
3) Doctrine of the Person of Christ, div. II, vol. I, p. 132.

ܐܓܪܬܐ ܕܡܪܝ، ܝܥܩܘܒ ܠܘܬ: ܐܣܛܦܢܐ ܒܪ ܨܘܕܝܠܐ[1]

ܫܦܝܪ ܠܟ ܕܪܗܛܬ ܐܝܬ ܒܒ̈ܢܝܐ ܕܫܦܝܪܬܐ ܐܘ ܪܚܡܐ[a] ܕܐܠܗܐ. ܘܡܢܐ ܠܟܣܝܢ ܦܪܘܫܘܬܐ[b] ܕܪܘܚܢܝܘܬܐ ܕܐܠܗܘܬܐ ܥܠܘܦ ܦܬܝܬܐ ܙܪܒ ܐܝܬ. ܒܠ ܡܒܪܐ ܕܐܠܗܐ. ܢܗܘܐ ܠܟ ܗܘܐ ܪܒ ܐܢܫܐ ܕܬܫܒܘܪ ܘܠܐ ܬܟܣܐ ܠܟ ܒܡ̈ܠܠܬܐ ܕܙܕܝܩܝܢ ܫܦܝܪܐ: ܐܒܪܐ ܠܢ ܡܢܐ ܕܙܪܒ. ܠܘ ܒܪܘܟܐ ܣܓܝܐ ܚܒܝܫܐ ܕܪܚܒܘܗܝ. ܐܠܐ *ܒܐܕܪܘܗܝ ܕܡܠܟܐ[c] ܛ̈ܠܠܬܐ. ܘܒܠ ܗ̇ܘ ܙܪܒ. ܒܠ ܕܢܒܥ ܛ̈ܠܠܬܐ. ܡܢܐ ܠܢ[d] ܕܐܪܓܫܬ ܢܦܫܐ ܒܡܠܟܐ ܚܕܬܐ: ܫܠܛܬ ܦܣܩܗ ܕܡܠܟܐ ܒܬܘܟܐ. ܘܒܗ ܪܫܝܡܐ ܡܒܪܪܐ ܠܗ ܠܗ ܒܠ ܦܘܩܕܐ. ܕܢܗܘܐ ܫܒܝܚ ܠܗ ܐܝܟ ܡܫܝܚܬܐ ܒܐܬܪܐ ܢܗܝܪܐ. *ܕܡܬܬܡܗܝܢ ܒܗ ܦ̈ܩܕܐ[e] ܠܒ̈ܢܝ ܦܬܝܬܐ. ܗܢܐ ܕܝܢ ܥܠܡܝܢ[f] ܥܠܝܐ. ܒܡܪܐ ܘܒܡܦܩܐ ܘܗܟܒܐ ܐܬܘܗܝ، ܦܬܠܠܐ ܗܘ[g] ܕܟܝܢܐ ܕܪܗܒ ܕܢܒܪ ܘܒܒܪܗ ܠܐܡܬܟܢܐ. ܦܩܫܐ ܫܐܢܐ ܗܘ ܫܦܝܪܐ ܕܢܓܠ[h] ܣܡܟܐ ܘܡܬܬܢܒܠ ܫܘܦܪܗ. ܒܡܘܬܗ ܠܢ[i] ܫܠܡܐ ܗܘ[k] ܘܚܝܝܢ ܣܘܦܐ ܕܓܠܐ. ܘܦܘܩܕܢ ܠܒ̈ܢܝܐ ܠܡܫܝ̈ܚܘܗܝ[l]

---

1) In the text, A, we follow Brit. Mus. Add. 14,587 (f. 1*a*), dated A. D. 603 (A. G. 914): as the beginning is wanting in this MS., it is supplied from B. M. Add. 17,163 (f. 23*b*). The various readings are taken 1) from the latter MS. marked B, also assigned to the VII cent.; 2) from C, the Vat. Syr. 107 (60, b, 1), which belongs to the VIII cent.; and 3) from D, the long extract in B. M. Add. 17, 193, dated A. D. 874 (f. 98). The title in C is ܬܘܒ ܕܝܠܗ ܕܗܘ ܕܝܠܗ ܕܡܪܝ، ܝܥܩܘܒ. ܕܠܘܬ ܐܣܛܦܢܐ ܒܪ ܨܘܕܝܠܐ.

a) C ܪܒܐ. *b*) C adds ܗ̇ܝ. *c*) C ܒܐܕܪ̈ܘܗܝ، ܕܡܠܟܡ. *d*) C omits. *e*) C ܕܡܬܬܡܗܝܢ ܒܗ ܦܬ̈ܝܬܐ *f*) C ܥܠܡܐ. *g*) C ܐܬܘܗܝ. *h*) C ܕܒܓܠ. *i*) C omits. *k*) C omits. *l*) B ܡܫܝ̈ܚܘܗܝ.

III.

LETTER OF MAR YA'QÛB TO STEPHEN BAR SUDAILI.

It is well for thee that thou walkest in glorious works, O friend of God, and it is honorable for thy intelligent soul that in the love of God thou sowest daily excellent things unto the hope of God, for the time will come that thou shalt reap: and be not anxious regarding the fruits of thy good sowing, for when the laborer sows he considers, in his mind's eye, not the seed but the furrows full of fruits; and for this does he sow, that he may gather the fruits. For, when the soul comprehends the new world, it despises the possessions of the old world and hastens to divide them among the needy, that they may be for it as a treasure in the abode of light, where good things are given to the workers of good. But this troubled world is as grass, hay, or flowers: it is a shadow which recedes and hastens to pass and remove the day-light (?); a lovely flower, whose beauty soon withers and perishes. Its riches are a dream and its possessions a deceptive vision. Error attaches to its posses-

ܐܝܟ ܫܡܥܬܐ ܕܥܠܡܐ: ܕܡܫܬܥܝܐ ܡܚܘܝܬܐ[a] ܠܗܘܢ *ܕܕܘܟܝܢ.
ܕܢܗܪܐ[b] ܒܫܡܥܬܐ ܕܠܝܬܘܗܝ[c]. ܘܡܢܐ ܕܐܬܬܚܪܝ[d] ܒܗܬ
ܘܡܬܬܘܐ. ܥܠ ܕܦܓܥܐ ܕܢܗܪܐ ܒܡܢܝܢܐ ܕܠܐ ܫܪܝܪ.
*ܐܬܬܚܪܪ ܐܬܬܚܪܪ[e] ܐܘ ܢܦܫܐ ܦܘܪܫܢܬܐ. ܘܠܫܪܝ ܒܘܫܢܐ
ܕܕܪܒܗ ܪܫܝܐ. ܒܪܘܫ[f] ܡܢ ܣܘܩܡܗ، ܦܘܪܫܢܐ ܕܠܠܐ.
ܘܒܬ، ܐܬܟܢܫܬ ܒܝܘܡܘܗܝ ܫܦܝܪܐ ܕܐܢܛܘܢܝܐ. ܫܢܝ، ܡܢܚ
ܡܫܝܚܐ ܕܗܘܐ ܠܗ ܫܠܝܚܐ؛ ܘܟܘܪ، ܠܦܘܠܘܣ ܡܫܠܡܢܘܬܐ
ܪ̈ܘܚܢܐ: ܕܒܫܠܡܘܬܐ ܩܪ̈ܝܫܐ ܗܘܝܐ ܒܗܬܝܪܐ: ܠܪ̈ܘܚܢ ܫܢܝܬܐ
ܡܠܬܐ ܥܠ ܬܘܒܢ. ܒܕܪ[g] ܠܗ ܠܠܐ ܘܡܬܦܪܫܝܢ ܫܠܝܡܘܗ̈ܝ.
ܡܫܬܪܐ ܠܗ ܥܠܡܐ ܘܡܬܒܣܪ̈ܝܢ[h] ܩܢܘܡܘܗ̈ܝ. ܘܠܦܘܡ[i]
ܕܐܒܠ ܣܘܟܐ. ܐܬܦܪܫܬ ܠܗ̇ ܒܝܘܡܘܗܝ ܕܪܘܡܐ. ܬ̇ܪܬ
ܒܟܘܪܐ ܘܫܘܠܦܢܐ ܕܐܬܠܬ ܡܢ ܐܝܠܝܢ ܕܢܕܝܒܬܐ. ܐܚܪܝܬ
ܠܗ̇ ܒܦܐܪܐ ܕܕܝܢ ܡܢ ܐܝܠܝܢ ܕܢ̈ܫܐ. ܐܚܪܝ، ܠܗ ܠܦܘܪܗ
ܕܦܪܘܣܐ. ܕܐܬܩܪܒܘ[k] ܠܗܘܢ ܐܦ̈ܠܝܕܐ[l] ܠܝܘܣܐ ܕܐܚܪܝܢ،
ܠܡܫܝܚܐ. ܪܡܙܗ ܕܪܘܒܐ ܥܒܠܐ ܗܘ، ܘܐܪܡܙܗ ܕܦܪܕܘܣܐ
ܦܬܝܟܐ ܗܘ، ܢܦܩܗ ܕܦܪ̈ܕܘܣܐ ܥܠ ܒܪܘܟܝܐ ܫܠܘ
ܢܝܚܐ ܠܒܢܝܐ؛ ܘܦܘܬܚܗ ܠܓܢܝܬܐ ܕܢܦܩܘ ܠܦܪܕܝܣܐ[m]
ܠܬܫܡܫܬܗܘܢ. ܘܦܪܐ ܐܝܟ ܚܒܪܐ ܡܢ ܫܒܝܐ. ܘܗܘܐ ܡܠܟܐ
ܠܥܠܡܐ. ܘܗܘܬ ܒܪܝܬܐ ܒܗ ܠܚܘܒܗ. ܕܠܐ ܐܢܫ ܢܬܪܓܪܓ
ܠܡܢܝܢܐ[n] ܠܐ ܡܬܩܪܒܢܐ[o]. ܠܐ ܠܡ ܬܘܒܢ ܕܒܗܘܢ[p] ܘܠܐ»
«ܡܘܡܐ ܘܠܐ ܚܫܟܐ ܒܡܫܝܚܘ ܘܠܐ ܬ̈ܪܬܝܢ ܩ̈ܕܡܝܢ»[q]

---

a) C ܡܚܘܝܢܐ. b) C ܕܢܗܘܝܐ. ܕܕܕܟܝܢ. c) C ܕܠܐ ܐܝܬܘܗܝ.
d) C ܕܐܬܬܚܪܪ. e) C ܐܬܬܚܪܪ، ܐܬܬܚܪܪ، f) C ܒܪܘܫ. g) C
ܒܕܪ. h) C ܘܡܬܒܣܪܝܢ. i) C ܘܠܦܘܡ. k) C ܕܐܬܩܪܒܘ.
l) C ܘܠܝܕܐ. m) With this word begins 14,587. n) C ܠܡܢܝܢܐ.
o) C ܡܬܩܪܒܢܐ. p) C ܠܐ ܕܒܗܘܢ. q) C ܩܕܡܝܢ.

sions, as to the treasure-trove of a dream, which in sleep enriches him who is asleep, so that he rejoices in a discovery which does not exist. When he awakes, he is ashamed and repents for making the mistake of rejoicing in unreal possessions. Awake! Awake! O prudent soul! put on the strength of the arm of the Lord: flee from the vain visions of the night, and come, rejoice in the beautiful light of day. Cast away from thee the possessions which dreams give unto thee, and despise error, the corrupter of minds, which in vain visions bestows wealth upon lovers of a sleep full of every harm. Night vanishes, dreams are exposed; the world passes away, and its riches are made vile; and error, which the serpent introduced, is exposed by the light of the Cross. The desire of wealth and power, which reigned from the tree of knowledge, has been destroyed by the fruit which dawned from the tree of life. The guardian of Paradise has been removed, that the keys of the Garden might be given to the thief who was deemed worthy of the right hand. The lance of the Cherub has been taken away and the way to Paradise is open. The planter of Paradise has been wounded by the lance in the place of the thieving gardener, and he has opened the garden that those who were expelled might return to their place. The great lawgiver descended from heaven, became the teacher of the world, and the creation was illuminated with his doctrine, (which is) that no man covet riches which he has not: „provide neither gold nor silver nor brass in your purses, neither two coats, nor

ܘܠܐ ܫܩܠ ܘܠܐ ܬܪܡܠܐ. ܘܫܠܡܐ ܕܐܢܫܐ ܒܐܘܪܚܐ»
ܠܐ ܬܫܐܠܘܢ». ܐܘܪܚܐ ܪܗܝܒܐ. *ܡܛܠ ܕܡܒܒܪ̈ܬܗ[a]
ܢܠܐ ܡܠܝܢ. ܚܪܘ ܦܘܣܘ ܡܢ ܫܠܡܐ. ܘܡܢ̈ܩܘܬܗ
ܠܐ ܬܬܚܫܒܘܢ. ܐܡܪ ܡܪܢܐ. ܠܐ ܬܬܝܨܦܘܢ ܕܡܚܪ ܣܦܩ»
ܠܗ ܠܝܘܡܐ ܒܝܫܬܗ. ܐܬܕܒܪ ܠܐܝܬܘܬܗ ܕܠܘܩܒܠ. ܘܐܙܠܘ»
ܪܗܛܐ. ܕܠܐ ܢܣܘܕܒܘܢ[b] ܫܠܡܐ ܒܒܢ̈ܬܗ. ܦܓܥ[c] ܒܗ
ܢܘܟܪܝܐ ܥܘܠܠܝܗ. ܡܫܡܫ ܐܝܬ ܒܗܘܬܐ ܕܐܘܢܣܝܗ. ܘܡܣܟܢܐ[d]
ܥܕ ܠܒܣܬܪܢ. ܒܥܘܠܠܝܐ ܠܐ ܬܫܘܪ ܒܗ. ܠܐܬܪܐ
ܘܒܡܥܪ̈ܬܐ[e] ܘܒܛܘܪ̈ܐ[f] ܗܘܘ ܢܒܪܝܐ. ܟܠܗ ܦܬܓܡܐ ܘܚܝܪܐ
ܠܢ. ܦܩܕ ܕܝ ܪܗܡܒ ܐܝܬ[g] ܠܚܘܒܐ ܥܒܝܕܐ. ܠܐ ܬܬܦܫܛ
ܠܢ ܦܣܩܬܐ ܒܐܪܥܐ. ܕܐܪܥܐ ܠܫܡܥܐ ܥܪܒܐ. ܠܥܩ̈ܒܐ
ܐܬܦܪܫܬ. ܒܐܪ̈ܥܢܘܬܐ ܠܐ ܬܬܚܢܫ. ܦܪ̈ܨܘܦܐ ܢܐܪ ܠܢ:
ܒܝܬ[h] ܒܩ̈ܒܐ ܡܢܝܐ ܚܕܐ ܐܝܬ. ܐܠܗܐ[i] ܠܕܝܢ ܡܢ ܡܢ̈ܝܐ
ܪܘܚܢܐ. ܘܒܕܡܘܬܐ ܕܒܝܬܗ ܪܒܢܝܢ. ܘܦܪܢ ܕܬܗܘܐ ܠܗ
ܢܬܬܐ. ܗܘ ܒܢܝܐ ܢܚܬܢ ܕܬܪܥܫ ܠܐܒܐ ܕܒܢܝܢ ܒܒܢ̈ܝܐ.
ܐܘ ܦܠܚ[k] ܐܝܟ ܐܓܪܐ. ܘܣܒ ܠܢ ܐܓܪܐ ܡܫܠܡܢܘܬܐ
ܕܫܡܫܐ: ܐܘ ܕܢܛܠ ܐܝܟ ܚܒܪܐ ܘܚܪܘܡ ܡܢ ܢܘܪܐ ܕܠܫܡܫܐ
ܠܡܫܡ̈ܫܢܐ. ܐܘ ܫܒܩ ܠܐܒܐ ܒܪ̈ܚܡܬܐ[l] ܕܒܢ̈ܝܐ. ܐܘ ܚ̈ܒܪ
ܠܒܢ̈ܬܐ ܕܬܪܬܐ[m] ܡܫܠܡܢܘܬܐ. ܐܘ ܗܘ ܒܫܬܐ ܕܬܬܦܝܐ ܡܢ
ܢܘܪܐ. ܒܡܒܒܪ̈ܬܐ ܠܒܢܝ ܕܢܘܪܐ. ܠܒܢܝܐ ܗܘ̈ܝܢ ܕܕܗܒܐ
ܠܒܢ̈ܕܝܣܝܢ. ܘܗܘ[n] ܦܣܩܬܐ ܕܣܝܡ ܒܝܬ ܠܒܢ̈ܐ. ܕܐܠܗܐܝܬ
ܒܒܢ̈ܝ ܘܠܗܘ[o] ܡܢ ܡܦܠܓ ܦܣܩܗ ܠܡܪ̈ܚܡܐ[p]. ܒܒܢ ܗܘܝܬ

a) C ܘܡܒܒܪ̈ܬܗ. b) B ܢܐܣܕܒܘܢ, c) B ܐܢ ܦܓܥ.
d) C ܘܡܣܟܢܐ. e) B ܕܒܡܥܪ̈ܬܐ, C ܐܦ ܠܡܥܪ̈ܬܐ. f) C omits.
g) C ܪܗܡܒܬ. h) BC ܒܝܬ. i) C ܐܠܗܢ. k) B ܦܠܚܘ.
l) BC ܒܪܚܡܬܐ. m) B ܕܬܪܬܬ. n) B ܘܠܗܘ. o) B ܠܗܘ, C ܠܗ. p) C ܠܡܪ̈ܚܡܐ.

stave, nor scrip; and salute no man by the way" [1]). The way is fearful, for its pathways are full of snares. Pass on! leave the world and be not taken up with its affairs. The Lord says: „Take therefore no thought for the morrow; sufficient unto the day is the evil thereof" [2]). Remember Lot's wife [3]) and hasten your course lest the world ensnare you with its evils. If beauty comes to thee, despise it: if thou findest riches, tread them under foot: cast possessions behind thee: look not after power: let thy country, thy house and thy family be strangers to thee. The Garden is open and awaits thee: advance in haste to the beautiful bride-chamber. Lay not up unto thyself a treasure upon earth [4]), for the earth is destined to destruction. Thou art called to heaven; give not thyself over to earthly things: paradise awaits thee; what willst thou among thorns? God begot thee of water and spirit, and brought thee up by the blood of His Son, and called thee to be His heir. Let thy nature move thee to love the Father who numbered thee among His sons. Oh! work like a laborer, and receive as thy wages the kingdom of Heaven. Oh! fear as a servant, and flee from the fire which threatens sinners. Minister unto the Father with a child's love. Do good, that thou mayest inherit the Kingdom: hate evil, that thou mayest be delivered from the fire. For on the fiery passage alms become a bridge to the givers of them, and he who has divided his possessions among the poor easily passes the gulf that is placed between the two sides.

1) Matthew X, 9: Luke X, 4: note transpositions and omissions.
2) From Matthew VI, 34.
3) Luke XVII, 32.
4) Matt. VI, 19.

ܠܡ [a] ܘܡܣܟܢܘܬܗܘܢ ܠܐ ܠܡܟܐܒ. ܘܢܓܗܐ ܗܘܬ ܘܐܫܬܡܥܘܬܗܘܢ.»
ܦܪܗܣܝܐ [b] ܗܘܬ ܘܡܫܪܪܘܬܗܘܢ. ܒܛܝܠܐ ܗܘܬ ܘܡܣܝܒܪܢܘܬܗܘܢ.»
ܘܒܬܪ ܐܡܝܪܐ [c] ܘܐܬܬܚܬܘ ܠܬܘ، ܘܡܠܠ ܥܠܝܗ ܗܘ ܟܠܡ»
ܒܪ̈ܚܡܘܗܝ، ܕܐܒܐ. ܡܛܠ ܗܝ ܠܐ ܡܬܥܪܦܠܐ ܠܗܕܐ ܒܪܬ
ܘܠܐ ܡܠܬ ܥܠ ܒܢ̈ܝܢܐ: ܘܡܬܪܗܒ ܕܢܝܪܐ ܘܒܕܪ *ܒܟܠܗ
ܡܣܝܡܗ [d] ܥܠ ܡܝ̈ܬܐ: ܕܢܚܒ ܡܢ ܐܠܗܐ ܕܐܡܪ ܠܗ ܗܘ ܐܬ
ܟܠܡ. ܐܘ *ܡܚܝܒ ܠܐ [e] ܕܢܠ ܘܐܝܟ [f] ܘܢܦܠ ܒܗ ܐܪܬܬܐ:
ܘܪܗܛ ܠܟܘܠܗܢܐ ܕܡܫܪܬܐ: ܕܠܐ ܢܬܢܠܦ ܒܗܠܝܢ ܕܡܬܐܡܪ [g]
ܠܗܘܢ ܡܢ ܕܢܪܐ ܕܢܣܒܐ: ܕܠܘ ܠܒܗܘܢ ܠܬܠܬܐ ܠܓܘܗܐ»
ܕܠܒܠܡ. ܣܬܪܐ [h] ܕܠܒܠܡ ܘܓܘܗܐ ܕܠܒܠܡ. ܠܐ ܠܣܬ̈ܪܐ
ܫܠܡܐ. ܘܠܐ ܠܓܘܗܐ ܦܣܩܐ. ܠܐ ܠܐܫܬܡܥܐ ܕܢܘܗܪܐ
ܕܐܝܬ [i] ܒܡܚܫܒܬܐ ܐܝܬ ܠܗ ܙܒܢܐ. ܘܠܐ ܠܦܘܢ ܠܚܫܘܟܐ [k]
ܬܪ̈ܝܢܐ [l] ܐܝܬ ܠܗ ܝܦܪܐ. ܒܐܠ [m] ܢܬܢܐ ܘܡܬܬܪܓܡ: ܬܪܒܗ
ܕܓܘܗܐ. ܘܠܐ ܦܬܚ ܠܕܢܚܝܢ. ܕܠܐ ܬܪܓܡܪ ܒܠܬܐ: ܒܒܕܢܐ
ܕܢܓܪ ܐܣܘܪܐ ܠܓܘܗܐ. ܬܪܒܨ ܕܒܘܠܐ [n] ܐܬܬܚܡ [o]. ܘܠܐ
ܦܬܚ ܢܘܗܪ [p] ܠܣܬ̈ܪܐ ܕܡܬܬܬܪܘ ܒܒܗܘܢ ܡܢ ܡܟܬ̈ܠܐ
ܬܦܢܝܐ [q]. ܒܗܐ ܕܐܬܓܪ ܕܢܐ ܠܐ ܡܗܘܐ ܦܣܩܐ. ܡܟܐ [r]
ܕܐܬܬܚܡ ܬܪܒܐ ܕܓܘܗܐ. ܠܐ ܦܬܚܐ ܒܠܬܐ ܠܡܬܢ̈ܕܐ [s].
ܡܪܢ ܡܪܢ ܦܬܚ ܠܢ. *ܡܬܦܢܝܢ ܗ̈ܘܝ ܠܗ: ܘܡܚܒܐ
ܗܘ [t] ܘܐܡܪ [u] ܠܗܘܢ. ܕܡܢ ܡܬܬܡܢ [v] ܠܐ ܝܕܥ ܐܢܐ ܠܟܘܢ.

---

a) C ܒܪܝ. *b*) C ܘܦܪܗܣܝܗ. *c*) BC insert ܗ̇ܘܬ. *d*) BC ܡܣܝܡܗ ܥܠܗ. *e*) B ܠܐ ܗܘ ܗ̇ܢ, C ܡܚܝܒ ܕܠܐ. *f*) B omits. *g*) C ܕܐܬܬܐܡܪ. *h*) C ܘܣܬ̈ܪܐ. *i*) C ܕܗܘܐܝܢ. *k*) C ܠܠܐ ܕܚܫܘܟܐ. *l*) C ܒ ܕܡܫܬܠܐ. *m*) C ܒܐܠ ܠܗ. *n*) B ܕܒܘܠܐ. *o*) C ܐܬܢܚ ܢܘܚ. *p*) C omits. *q*) C ܡܟܬ̈ܠܐ ܬܦܢܝܐ. *r*) B ܘܡܟܐ. *s*) C inserts ܐܡܪܝܢ. *t*) C omits. *u*) C ܐܡܪ. *v*) C ܕܡܬܬܡܢ, C ܡܬܬܡܢ.

„For I was an hungered and ye gave me meat: I was thirsty and ye gave me drink: I was sick and ye visited me: naked and ye clothed me. I was in prison and ye came unto me. Therefore come in peace, ye blessed of my Father" [1]). Who would not long for this word so full of every consolation, and hasten to disperse and distribute among the needy all his possessions, that he may hear God saying unto him, "Come in peace"? And who is there that would not fear and be filled with terror and trembling and hasten to do good works, lest he be joined unto those to whom the terrible Judge says: „Depart, ye cursed, into everlasting hell". Life everlasting, and hell everlasting: there is no end to life, and no termination to hell. To the day-light which is on the right hand there is no evening, and to the outer night-darkness on the left there is no morning.

The bridegroom enters and the door of the bride-chamber is closed, and is not opened unto those who knock, lest the bride be covered with shame at the time when the honor of the bride-chamber should be guarded [2]). Noah closed the door of the ark and opened it not unto fornicators that they might be protected with him from the great deluge. When judgment has been rendered, supplication is of no avail. When the door of the bride-chamber has been closed, the bride [3]) will not open unto the invited guests who entreat, saying: „Lord, Lord, open unto us". But He answers and says unto them: „I know you not at all" [2]). He did not

---

1) From Matthew XXV, 34–35.

2) From Matthew XXV, 10–12.

3) Here ܟܠܬܐ seems to be a mistake of the copyist for ܚܬܢܐ „the bridegroom".

ܠܘ ܠܐ[a] ܦܬܚ ܐܢܐ ܠܟܘܢ ܒܠܚܘܕ ܐܡܪ[b]. ܐܠܐ ܕܐܦܠܐ
ܡ̣ܕܒܪܢܐ[c] ܠܟܘܢ: ܦܫܛ ܫܘܬܐ ܠܡܫܠܡܘܬܐ. ܕܕܒܪ ܒܢܝܢܟܘܢ
ܢܘܗܪܐ ܕܠܡܫܬ̈ܪܝܘܬܟܘܢ[d]. ܠܐ ܠܡ ܡ̣ܕܒܪ ܐܢܐ ܠܟܘܢ. ܒܐܡܬ
ܠܐ ܬܬܠܐܝܢ ܒܦܘܫܩܐ ܕܠܐ ܡܬܦܫܩ. ܠܐ ܬܬܥܝ̈ܩܢ[e]
ܡܛܠܗܘܢ ܕܫܘܬܐ: ܒܒܪܢܐ ܕܫܦܪ ܒܗ ܐܡܘܪܐ[f] ܠܫܠܡܘܬܐ[g].
ܐܡܒܪ[h] ܬܘܒܢܐ ܕܠܡܫܬܪܝܢܟܘܢ[d] ܕܒܬܒܐ: ܡܢ ܬܪܥܐ ܕܒܫܬ
ܚܘܒܐ: ܕܒܘܗܪܐ ܕܫܒܝܚܘܬܐ ܗܘܐ ܕܘܪܫ[i] ܡܫܝܚܐ ܒܡ
ܫܘܬܐ ܒܡܫܡܫܗ[k]. «ܬܘ ܒܫܠܡ ܒܪ̈ܝܟܘܗܝ ܕܐܒܝ. ܬܘ ܒܫܠܡ»
«ܒܢ̈ܝ ܕܢܘܗܪܐ. ܬܘ ܒܫܠܡ ܡܬܪ̈ܣܝܢ[l] ܠܡܫܬܘܬܐ. ܬܘ ܒܫܠܡ»
«ܕܒܪ ܫܘܒܚܐ[m]. ܬܘ ܐܪܬܘ[n] ܡܠܟܘܬܐ ܕܠܟܘܢ ܡܛܝܒܐ:»
«ܡܛܠ ܫܘܦܪܐ ܕܒܪ̈ܝܬܟܘܢ ܒܟܢܫܐ[o]. ܘܠܐ ܠܟܘܢ ܠܒܢ ܠܬܠܐ»
«ܠܢܘܗܪܐ[p] ܕܠܡܠܐ ܠܥܠܡ ܥܡܪܐ ܘܠܡܠܟܘܬܗܘܢ ܫܘܬܦܘܬܗ[q].»
«ܕܫܠܡܬܐ[r] ܗܝ ܪܒܬܐ ܠܟܠ ܒܐܪ̈ܚܘܗܝ ܕܐܠܗܐ ܚܝܐ.»
ܡܫܠܡܘܬܐ ܗܝ ܕܡܠܝܐ ܒܟܠܗ̇ ܫܦܝܘܬܐ[s]: ܕܒܢ̈ܝܫܐ[t] ܕܘܟܝܐ
ܘܢܘܗܪܐ ܕܡܬܒܠ ܐܝܟ: ܒܟܠ[u] ܠܥܡܝܐ ܕܠܝܬ ܠܗ̇ ܫܘܠܡܐ.
ܫܠܘ̈ܐ ܐܬܦܠܣܘ ܒܡܫܝܚܐ[v] ܡܕܒܪܐ ܕܡܫ̈ܡܫܢܐ ܘܢܘܗܪܐ.
ܘܡܫܡܫ ܒܦܐܪ ܕܠܡܘܢ ܡܬܦܪܫ[w] ܕܠܐ[x] ܡܫܝܚܐ ܕܡܫ̈ܡܫܢܘܬܐ
*ܒܪ ܫܡܫܐ[y]. ܕܠܝܬ[z] ܬܡܢ ܐܫܬܡܫܐ ܘܠܠܝܘܬܐ. ܘܐܬܒܪܟ[aa]

---

a) B ܠܘ ܕܠܐ. b) B ܐܡܪ. c) B ܡ̣ܕܒܪ ܐܢܐ. d) C ܕܠܡܫܬ̈ܪܝܢܟܘܢ.
e) B ܬܬܥܝ̈ܩܢ. f) C ܐܡܘܪ̈ܐ. g) C inserts ܐܡܪ ܠܗܘܢ.
h) B ܐܡܒܪ̈ܝܢ. i) C ܘܕܪܫ. k) C inserts ܘܐܡܪ ܠܗܘܢ. l) C
ܡܬܪ̈ܣܝܢ. m) C inserts ܬܘ ܒܫܠܡ ܦܠܚ̈ܝ ܟܪܡܐ.. n) C ܐܪܬܘ.
o) C inserts ܐܡܪ ܠܗܘܢ ܕܡܢ ܫܡܝܐ. p) C inserts ܗ̇ܝ. q) C
ܫܘܬܦܘ̈ܬܗ. r) Here begins the extract in Add. 17,193. s) D
ܫܦܝܘܬܐ. t) CD ܕܒܢ̈ܝܫܐ. u) C ܕܒܟܠ. v) C erron. ܒܢ̈ܝܫܐ.
w) C omits. x) C ܠܝܬ ܠܗ. y) C correctly ܘܫܪ̈ܝܐ. z) C
ܠܝܬ. aa) C ܘܒܪܟ.

say, I will not open unto you, but „I know you not". The bridegroom answered the foolish virgins, who had willingly allowed the light of their lamps to go out, „I know you not"; that is: „Raise not your supplications, for they will not be accepted; defile not the chamber of the bridegroom when the honor of the bride should be guarded therein; remove the smoke of your extinguished lamps from the door of the bride-chamber, for behold the guests who are with the bridegroom in the guest-chamber are illuminated with the lights of the wise virgins. Come in peace, ye blessed of my Father; come in peace, ye givers of alms; come in peace, ye feeders of the poor; come in peace, ye sowers of good works; come, inherit the kingdom prepared for you on account of the excellence of your good deeds. Depart, ye cursed, into the fire prepared for the devil and all his ministers" [1]. „It is a most terrible thing to fall into the hands of the living God" [2]. It is an offence full of foolishness that, for the enjoyments of a short while, a man should be led into entering hell, to which there is no end. They work iniquities during a certain small number of days, but their torments have no limit of days or years, for *there* are no days or nights. Perhaps thou wilt say: How can a just judge, for

1) A paraphrase of Matthew XXV, 34—41.
2) Hebrews X, 31.

ܬܐܡܪ ܕܐܝܟܢ[a] ܕܐܝܢܐ ܒܐܝܢܐ: ܣܠܩ ܣܗܪ̈ܐ ܕܡܬܦܠܓܝܢ
ܒܥܡ̈ܡܐ ܥܒܪ̈ܝܢ: ܐܘ ܒܥܡܡܝܢ ܐܘ ܒܥܡܡܐ ܕܗܘܐ ܥܒܪܝܐ. ܟܕ
ܕܐܝܢܐ ܕܠܥܠܡ. ܕܢܦܠ[b] ܒܫܘܠܡܐ ܗܘ ܕܫܠܝܐ. ܐܡܪܝܢ ܗܘ
ܕܐܝܢܐ ܘܬܪܓܡ ܕܒܢ̈ܘܗܝ ܐܘ[c] ܪܗܛ ܬܪܓܡܢܘܬܐ. ܐܠܐ ܒܪ[d]
ܒܐܝܢܐ ܕܠܫܠܝܐ ܕܐܒܢܐ ܘܒܢܝܐ: ܢܚܕܐ[e] ܒܫܘܪܝܐ ܕܠܥܠܡ
ܐܝܟ ܕܐܬܒ. ܐܦ ܠܐ ܒܐܝܢܐ ܗܘܬ ܕܠܗܘ ܕܡܫܪܪܝܢ ܒܗܢܐ
ܘܒܘܪܐ: ܢܘܪܬ ܡܠܟܘܬܐ ܕܠܥܠܡ. ܘܗܘ ܐܝܟ ܒܐܝܢܘܬܐ[f] ܢܚܒܢܐ
ܠܝ: ܕܠܗܘܬܐ[g] ܡܫܝܚܘܬܐ ܕܝܠܝܕܐ ܕܫܠܝܐ ܒܗܝܢ ܫܠܝܐ
ܢܬܬܕܡ[h] ܒܠܫܢܐ. ܡܛܠ ܬܘܕܝܬܐ ܐܦ ܗܝ ܕܠܗܘܬ[g] ܡܫܝܚܘܬܐ
ܕܫܡܥܐ ܕܐܘܕܝܬ[i] ܒܗܝܢ ܘܕܡܟܐ ܢܬܒܣܡ ܒܠܫܢܐ. ܘܗܘ
ܕܒܚܡܫ ܥܣܪܝܢ ܫܠܝܐ ܢܗܘܐ ܒܘܪܐ ܒܚܡܫ ܥܣܪܝܢ ܒܠܫܢܐ.
ܘܗܘ ܕܒܠܫ ܘܕܡܘܬܐ ܒܚܡܫ ܥܣܪܝܢ. ܬܘܒ ܐܡܘܬܗ ܢܗܘܐ
ܒܡܠܟܘܬܐ *ܒܚܡܫ ܥܣܪܝܢ ܒܠܫܢܐ[k] ܦܘܩܕܢ. ܐܝܟ[l] ܕܒܪ[m]
ܒܐܝܢܐ ܗܝ[n]. ܐܦ ܗܕܐ ܬܪܓܡܐ. ܡܛܠ ܕܚܘܫܒܐ ܒܪ ܡܫܝܚܐ.
ܚܕܐ ܫܒܬܐ ܒܠܫܢܐ ܗܘܐ ܒܝܬ ܟܕܡ[o]. ܡܛܠ ܕܚܕܐ
ܫܒܬܐ ܒܠܫܢܐ ܬܪܬܝܢ ܒܡܫܡܫܢܘܬܐ: ܒܪ ܡܫܝܚܐ ܠܡܫܝܚܐ
ܕܬܕܒܪܗ ܒܡܠܟܘܬܐ[p]: ܠܐ ܗܕܝܐ ܐܘ ܫܒܪܐ ܠܐ ܗܕܝܐ.
ܠܘ ܐܝܟ ܪܚܝܩ ܕܠܝ: ܡܬܦܪܫ ܕܒܢܝܐ ܬܪܓܡܐ ܕܐܠܗܐ
ܒܐܝܢܐ[q]. *ܗܠܝܢ[r] ܠܗܝ[s] ܠܢܘܪܐ ܕܠܥܠܡ. ܘܕܡܝܐ ܠܫܡ̈ܐ
ܕܠܥܠܡ. ܫܠܝܐ ܕܠܐ ܬܐܒ ܠܥܠܡ ܐܠܐ ܚܕܐ. ܠܥܠܡ *ܫܠܝܐ

---

a) D ܕܐܝܟܢܐ. *b*) C ܢܦܠ. *c*) AD read erron. ܐܦ. *d*) D omits. *e*) C ܢܚܬܕܐ. *f*) B ܟܝܢܘܬܐ, C ܒܐܝܢܐܝܬ. *g*) D inserts ܗܝ. *h*) BC ܢܬܕܡ. *i*) D ܕܐܘܕܝܬܘܢ. *k*) C omits. *l*) C ܐܘܟ. *m*) BCD correctly insert ܗܝ. *n*) B omits. *o*) C ܟܕܡ. *p*) B ܒܡܠܟܘܬܗ. *q*) B omits. *r*) C inserts ܐܠܐ ܐܡܪ ܗܕܐ. ܕܗܠܝܢ. *s*) C omits.

sins committed during ten, twenty or a like number of years, condemn the sinner to fall forever into hell? But the judge is just and his judgments righteous, thou lover of rectitude; for if it be not just that He should cast into everlasting fire him who has sinned during a short time, as is written; then also is it not just that He should cause him who has been righteous during a short time to inherit the everlasting kingdom. And if it seems to thee that the sinner should be judged according to the number of years during which he has sinned, it would then follow that the righteous should enjoy happiness also according to the number of years during which he practised righteousness. So that he who sinned during ten years would remain in the fire for only ten, and he who practised righteousness for ten years would also remain in the kingdom for only ten years and would then leave it.

If the first (proposition) be just, and the second also right (in consequence), then the thief who was on the right hand could have been but a single hour in the Garden of Eden, for he burned with faith but for an hour when he besought Christ to remember him in his kingdom.

It is not so, friend, it is not so; not according to thine opinion is the righteous judgment of the just God governed, (which is) that these should go into eternal firo, and the righteous into eternal life. The sinner who repents not, if he had lived forever, would have sinned forever, and

ܗܘܐ[a]. ܘܠܒܬܪ ܢܦܩܐ ܕܪܒܝܢܗ[b] ܕܐܬܬܡܫ ܥܠ ܫܠܝܚܘܬܐ:
*ܢܦܠ ܒܟܪܝܘܬܐ[c] ܓܘܢܐ ܕܒܠܥܡ. ܗܘ ܓܝܪ ܒܬܪܐ *ܕܥܠܬܐ
ܗܘܐ[d] ܡܫܡܫܢܘܗܝ, ܕܠܠܝܬܐ ܡܫܒܚܬܐ. ܗܘ[e] ܐܡܪ ܠܢܦܫܗ[f]:
ܐܒܘܠܢ ܐܬܚܪܝ ܐܬܟܫܦ. ܐܢܬ ܠܗ ܕܠܠܝܬܐ ܡܫܒܚܬܐ.»
ܕܢܦܪܘܢ ܠܒܢܝܐ ܡܫܒܚܬܐ«: *ܘܗܢܐ ܕܗܘ[g] ܡܛܠ ܪܒܝܢܗ:
*ܕܡܫܒܚܬܐ ܥܢܝܢܐ ܢܣܒܬ[h] ܘܐܬܟܫܦܘ[i] ܚܝܠܘܗܝ, ܘܠܐ
ܐܬܟܫܦܬ[k] ܫܠܝܚܘܬܗ. ܡܛܠ[l] ܕܦܩܕ[m] ܡܛܠ ܪܒܝܢܗ: ܕܠܒܠܡ
ܢܬܟܫܦ ܒܢܝܫܐ[n]. ܘܒܐܝܘܬܐ[o] ܗܝ, ܗܕܐ *ܕܗܘܝܐ ܠܒܠܡ
ܢܬܕܡ[p]. ܥܠ ܕܡܫܒܚܝܢ ܠܒܠܡ ܒܢܝܘܬܗ[q] ܚܝܐ ܗܘܐ.
ܗܒܝܠ ܐܦ *ܪܒܝܢܗ ܕܕܘܝܐ ܠܒܠܡ ܦܠܚ ܠܐܠܗܐ
ܡܫܒܚܝܢ[r]. *ܐܦ ܐܢ[s] ܚܝܘܗܝ, *ܕܠܐ ܡܫܒܚܝܢ[t] ܦܫܩ ܠܗܘܢ
ܡܘܬܐ ܡܢ ܪܘܓܙܐ ܕܕܘܝܘܬܐ. ܘܦܩܕ ܠܚܠܬ, ܗܘ ܒܬܪ[u]
ܒܫܘܝܐ ܐܘܟܝ. ܗܕ ܓܝܪ ܒܪܝ ܒܠܗܘ, ܥܘܝܢܐ: ܘܐܬܚܒܠ
ܦܓܪܗ ܒܒܐܝܬܐ ܡܪܝܪܐ: ܘܐܬܚܝܠ ܚܝܠܘܬܐ ܕܓܘܫܡܗ
ܒܟܘܕܪܐ: ܘܐܬܟܫܦܘ[v] ܗܕܡܘܗܝ, ܡܢ ܪܘܓܙܐ ܕܟܝܢܘܬܗ.
ܗܘ[w] ܐܡܪ ܗܘܐ ܒܒܝܘܬܐ ܕܒܐܒܗ. ܕܒܕܝܐ ܕܐܟܝܢܘܬ»
ܠܐ ܬܒܥܪ ܬܡܟܡܟܘܬ, ܡܕܝ. ܘܒܕܘܝܘܬ, ܐܢܫܡܫ ܘܠܐ«

---

a) C ܗܘ ܫܠܝܚܐ. b) C inserts ܕܫܠܝܚܐ. c) B ܒܟܪܝܘܬ ܢܦܠ, C ܒܟܪܝܘܬ ܢܦܠ. d) C ܕܓܒܠܐ ܒܝܬ. e) C ܗܒܝܢܐ. f) C inserts ܢܦܫܗ:. g) C ܘܗܒܝܢܐ. h) B ܕܥܢܝܢܐ ܡܫܒܚܬܐ ܢܣܒܬ, C ܕܥܢܝܢܐ ܘܥ ܢܬܟܫܦ. i) BD ܐܬܟܫܦܘ. k) BD ܐܬܟܫܦܬ: B adds ܗܝ. l) C ܘܡܛܠ. m) C ܕܗܒܝܢܐ. n) D ܒܢܝܫܐ. o) B ܘܒܝܘܬܐ, C ܒܝܘܬܐ. p) C ܕܢܬܕܡ ܗܘܐ ܒܝܘܪܐ ܕܠܒܠܡ. q) C ܒܡܒܝܘܬܐ. r) C ܕܕܘܝܐ ܒܡܪܥܝܬ ܢܦܠ ܚܝܐ ܕܠܒܠܡ. ܥܠ ܕܡܫܒܚܝܢ ܠܒܠܡ ܚܝ ܕܦܠܚ ܠܐܠܗܐ. s) BC ܐܦ. t) C omits but inserts after ܡܘܬܐ. u) C ܬܗܪܝ. v) C ܘܐܬܟܫܦܘ. w) BC ܗܒܝܢܐ.

according to the inclination of his mind to continue in sin he justly falls into everlasting hell. For the rich man who filled his barns with many fruits said thus unto his soul: „Eat, drink, and be merry; thou hast much goods laid up for many years" [1]. And thus his mind was bent on making merry for many years; his life therefore is cut off, but not his sin, for his mind was bent upon giving itself up to enjoyments forever. It is therefore justice which condemns this man to eternal fire, for, as far as his will was concerned, he would have lived forever in gluttony. Thus also the righteous man justly inherits eternal life, because, as far as his will was concerned, he contemplated serving God forever, although his life was, beyond his control, cut off by death from the course of righteousness. Job also, so admirable in the midst of temptations, is my witness; for, while he was attacked with ulcers and his body was corrupted with sore boils, the ulcers of his body mingled together, and his members made putrid by the discharge from his sores, he spoke thus in the intensity of his anguish: "Until I die mine integrity shall not depart from me. My righteousness I hold fast and will not let it go" [2], and

1) Luke XII, 19.

2) Job XXVII, 5–6: »and mine integrity etc.", an erroneous repetition

ܐܬܪܦܐ[a]. ܘܐܠܘ ܠܐ ܬܥܒܪ ܬܫܡܫܬܗ܆ ܡܢܗ». ܘܠܗܘܢܐ
ܪܥܝܢܐ ܠܒܝܫܐ: ܕܗܘܡ[b] ܡܬܚܫܒ ܗܘܐ ܥܠ ܪܗܛܐ
ܕܙܘܕܡܘܬܐ. *ܐܝܟܐ ܗܘ[c] ܕܢܚܐ ܕܠܐ ܡܕܡ ܠܗ[d] ܡܠܝܘܬܐ
ܕܠܟܠܗ: ܕܢܗܘܐ ܒܗ ܕܠܐ ܫܘܠܡܐ. ܡܕܝܢ ܫܦܪ ܠܝ[e]
ܠܡܐܡܪ. ܕܙܘܕܡ ܐܢܬ ܡܕܝܢܐ ܘܥܠ ܦܬܓܡܝ ܕܬܠܡܝܕܢ. ܘܪܡܙܐ[f]
ܒܐܘܪܚܬܟ[g] ܡܢ ܒܕܠܝܐ. ܘܬܪܥܝ ܐܘܪܚܬܟ ܘܠܝܬ ܒܗܝܢ
ܬܘܩܠܬܐ. ܘܒܐܝܢܐܝܬ[h] ܢܥܠ ܣܦܝܢܐ ܒܢܘܪܐ ܕܠܟܠܗ: ܡܛܠ
ܕܡܬܚ ܫܘܒܚܗ، ܕܠܟܠܗ ܣܦܝܢܐ: ܘܠܐ ܐܬܦܢܝ ܠܬܝܒܘܬܐ.
ܘܫܩܠ ܙܘܕܐ ܠܚܝܠܐ ܕܠܟܠܗ:[i] ܡܛܠ ܕܢܦܩܘ ܢܦܫܗܘܢ
ܘܟܝܢܗܘܢ ܕܠܟܠܗ ܢܦܪܩܘܢ ܒܐܘܪܚܐ ܕܙܘܕܡܘܬܐ. ܠܝ ܕܝܢ
ܗܫܐ[k] ܫܦܪ ܠܝ. ܕܐܝܟ ܕܟܬܒܐ ܐܢܬ ܠܝ. ܢܘܪܒ[l] ܦܬܓܡܐ.
ܘܡܕܪܫܐ ܦܘܪܥܢܐ ܪܒܐ ܡܢ ܦܘܠܚܢܐ ܕܒܪܐ. ܡܢ ܪܗܛܐ
ܫܪܝܐ ܕܟܠܠ ܫܘܩܠܬܐ. ܡܠܟܘܬܐ ܕܫܡܝܐ ܕܠܝܬ ܠܗ̇
ܫܘܠܡܐ: ܘܕܢܚܘܪܘܢ[m] ܡܢ ܫܢܝܐ[n] ܕܚܝܐ ܘܒܪܐ: ܕܠܐ
ܢܥܒܕ ܡܢܗܘܢ ܦܘܪܥܢܐ[o] ܕܠܟܠܗ. ܐܢܬ ܕܝܢ ܐܘ ܚܒܪܐ
ܕܐܠܗܐ. ܐܝܟ ܪܗܛܐ ܒܬܪ ܫܦܝܪܘܬܐ. ܘܦܠܚ ܕܒܥܬܟ
ܕܬܫܬܡܫ[p] ܠܡܕܡܝܟ. ܘܠܐ ܢܗܡ ܥܠ ܪܥܝܢܟ ܗܠܝܢ[q]
ܦܬܓܡܐ ܕܟܬܒܬ ܠܟ. ܕܠܐ ܢܬܦܠܠܘܢ ܡܢ ܗܠܝܢ *ܕܟܬܒܬ:
ܐܢܬ[r] ܠܡܟܬܒ. ܐܠܐ ܥܠ ܗܝܟܐ ܕܕܚܝܠ ܠܝ ܫܡܫܐ.
ܫܘܪܝܐ ܕܝܢ ܠܦܘܪܫܢܐ ܕܡܕܝܢ ܐܢܬ. ܘܥܠ ܗܕܐ ܚܝܪ ܓܒܪܐ

---

a) B ܐܪܦܐ. b) C ܕܗܘܝܢܐ. c) BC ܐܝܟܢ. d) D inserts ܗܝ. e) B ܗܫܐ. f) B inserts ܗܝ. g) B ܒܐܘܪܚܟ. h) BC ܘܒܐܝܢܐܝܬ. i) Here ends extract D (Add. 17,193). k) C omits ܗܫܐ. l) BC ܕܢܘܪܒ. m) BC ܘܢܚܘܪܘܢ. n) BC ܫܢ̈ܝܐ. o) C ܦܘܪܥܢܐ. p) BC ܘܬܫܬܡܫ. q) C omits. r) C ܕܟܬܒܬ.

mine integrity shall never depart from me. What judge would not award the everlasting kingdom to this steadfast mind, thus bent on the course of righteousness that he might live forever!

Therefore it is meet for us to say, "Righteous art thou, O Lord, and upright are thy judgments [1]), and thy righteousness is above all blame. Thy ways are upright [2]) and in them are no stumbling-blocks". Justly does the sinner fall into fire everlasting, because his thoughts were bent on sinning for ever, neither did he turn unto repentance. The righteous also are worthy of eternal life, because they devoted their souls and minds to walk forever in the way of righteousness.

We ought, however, while we yet have time, to sow good works, that we may receive a great recompense for but little labor; for an excellent life of but few days, the kingdom of heaven which has no end. (We ought) to flee from pleasures of short duration, lest through them we bring upon ourselves eternal torments. But thou, O pious man, hasten thy course after excellent things: "forget what is behind thee, and strive after what is before thee" [3]). Let not the good thou hast done dwell upon thy mind, lest it prevent thee from doing what thou hast still to do. But every day that the sun rises upon thee make a beginning of goods works to do them, and every day complete them,

---

1) Psalm CXIX, 137.
2) Cf. Psalm CXLV, 17. Revel. XV, 3.
3) Philip. III, 13.

ܘܠܥܠܡ ܠܐ ܬܫܬܠܐ[a]. ܘܡܬܬܢܝܚ ܩܕܡܝܐ[b] ܕܪܚܡܝܢ. ܕܕܠܐ
ܫܠܡܐ ܬܗܘܐ ܥܠܝܟ ܦܬܟܪܐ. ܡܛܠ ܕܠܡܠܟܘܬܐ[c] ܕܠܥܠܡ
ܕܠܝܬ ܠܗ ܫܘܠܡܐ. ܡܛܪܦܬܐ ܐܝܬ ܕܬܥܒܕ. ܘܗܘܝ[d] ܪܒܐ
ܘܐܝܟ ܘܕܝܠ ܡܢ ܢܘܪܐ ܕܠܥܠܡ[e] ܕܠܐ ܫܢܝܢ ܠܡܫܡܠܝܐ:
ܕܬܪܕܘܢ[f] ܒܕܒܝܬܐ ܕܠܝܬ ܠܗ ܫܘܠܡܐ. ܘܗܘܐ ܫܪܪܐ
ܒܪܚܡܝܢ. ܗܘ ܒܪܬ ܩܠܐ ܕܕܝܢܐ ܕܢܦܠܐ ܕܐܡܪ[g]: «ܕܬܐܪܬܘܢ
ܗܠܝܢ ܠܢܘܪܐ ܕܠܥܠܡ. ܘܕܝܢܐ ܠܚܝܐ ܕܠܥܠܡ.»
ܕܗܘܝ[h] *ܒܠܒܘܬܗ ܘܒܪܚܡܘܗܝ[i]: ܢܦܘܩ ܕܬܗܘܐ
ܫܠܝܛ ܐܝܬ[k] ܒܗܠܝܢ ܕܡܬܐܡܪܝܢ[l] ܠܗܘܢ: «ܕܒܩܡ
ܗܘܝܬ ܘܡܬܒܗܬܘܢ ܠܐ ܠܡܬܒܥܐ: ܘܝܩܪܐ»
ܗܘܝܬ ܘܐܫܬܘܕܥܢ. ܘܒܫܒܗܘܢ
ܬܬܬܩܢܢ ܒܐܬܪܐ ܕܢܘܗܪܐ.
ܒܚܝܐ ܕܠܥܠܡ ܥܠܡܝܢ[m]
ܐܡܝܢ ܀
ܫܠܡܬ ܀

---

a) BC ܬܫܬܠܡ. b) C ܕܪܚܡܗ. c) C ܡܠܟܘܬܐ. d) C ܗܘܝ. e) B inserts ܗܝ. f) C ܕܬܪܕܘܢ. g) BC ܕܐܡܪܐ. h) B inserts ܡܪܢ. i) C ܒܪܚܡܘܗܝ. k) C ܫܠܝܛܬ. l) C ܕܐܬܐܡܪܝܢ. m) C omits ܥܠܡܝܢ.

neither cease forever. Direct the faculties of thy mind so that without ceasing they do good works. As thou desirest to enter into the eternal kingdom which has no end, reflect, tremble, and fear the everlasting fire prepared for the wicked, who will be condemned by a judgment which has no end. Let this word of the terrible judge be present in thy mind which saith: "These shall go into fire everlasting, and the righteous unto life everlasting" [1]. May He by His goodness and love make thee worthy to be numbered among those to whom it is said, "I was an hungered and ye gave me meat, I was thirsty and ye gave me drink", and with them mayest thou be a guest in the abode of light in life everlasting. Amen.

1) Matthew XXV, 46.

ܐܓܪܬܐ ܕܡܪܝ ܐܟܣܢܝܐ ܕܡܒܘܓ܆
ܠܘܬ ܐܒܪܗܡ ܘܐܘܪܣܛܐ ܩܫܝ̈ܫܐ ܕܐܘܪܗܝ܆
ܡܛܠ ܣܛܦܢܐ ܒܪ ܨܘܕܝܠܝ ܐܘܪܗܝܐ[1] ܀

ܣܛܦܢܐ ܡܫܢܝܐ ܗ̇ܘ ܕܩܕܡ ܕܒܢܐ ܐܙܠ ܡܢ ܠܘܬܢ܆ ܘܟܬܒ
ܗܢܐ ܒܐܬܪܐ ܕܐܘܪܫܠܡ܆ ܠܘܬ ܕܐܢ̈ܫܐ ܕܝܠܗ ܫܕܪ
ܠܘܬܟܘܢ ܡܕܡ ܡܠܝܠ ܣܘܟ̈ܬܐ܆ ܒܗ ܐܓܪ̈ܬܐ ܘܟܬ̈ܒܐ
ܕܣܘ̈ܟܠܗܝ. ܒܗ̇ ܦܘܩܐ ܠܗ ܥܡܠ ܛܒܒܐ ܕܬܬܟܫܦܐ ܡܢ
ܡܟܬܒܬܐ ܕܗ̇ܢܝ ܕܐܫܬܕܪܘ. ܘܗ̇ܘ ܡܕܡ ܕܢܘܪܒܐܬ ܐܓܠܒ
ܕܢܦܫܗ: ܐܡܪ ܓܒܪ ܕܐܢܫܘ ܕܫܠܘܦ ܐܢܐ ܕܫܠܝܛ ܐܢܫ̈ܐ
ܠܘܬܟܘܢ: ܘܕܫܕܪ ܐܦ ܒܟܬ̈ܒܐ܆ ܡܬܕܒܪ ܠܗ ܒܒܪ ܣܒܪܗ.
ܓܕܐ ܓܒܪ ܡܢ ܐܒܗ̈ܐ ܠܐ ܢܦܩ ܐܢܐ: ܡܕܒܪܐ ܕܝܢ ܕܡܢ
ܣܛܢܐ: ܗܘܘ ܓܒܪ ܐܬܘܗܝ܆ ܐܒܐ ܘܒܠܬܐ ܕܟܠ ܗܪ̈ܣܝܣ.
ܕܢܓܠܐ ܒܟܬܒܐ ܣܘܠܦܢܐ ܪܘܚܢܐ ܘܫܒܠܐ. ܗ̇ܘ ܕܠܘ ܒܠܫܢܐ
ܗܪܣܝܣ ܦܠܐ ܕܢܬܚܫܒ. ܐܠܐ ܘܕܟܝܪ ܡܢ ܣܘܦܘܬܐ
ܘܡܣܪܗܒܘܬܐ. ܗܘ ܕܓܠܝܢܐܝܬ ܟܣܝܐ ܒܪܘܚܐ ܠܐܠܗܐ.
ܘܡܬܚܐ ܕܟܠܡܕܡ ܢܗܘܐ ܐܠܗܘܬܗ. ܘܡܬܕܟܠ ܬܘܒ ܠܟܬ̈ܒܐ
ܡܕ̈ܢܚܐ. ܘܦܫܩ ܡܫܪܐ ܐܦ ܟܠ ܦܘܪܫܢܘܬܐ. ܘܡܚܠܦ ܠܟܠ
ܟܪܝܗܐ ܕܢܗܘܐ ܟܡܐ ܕܗܘܝܐ. ܘܟܠܗ ܡܢ ܬܘܠܡܕܐ ܘܡܢ
ܕܢܦܩܐ ܠܘܬ ܐܠܗܐ. ܐܦ ܠܫ̈ܐܕܐ ܘܡܪ̈ܘܕܐ ܘܗܪ̈ܛܝܩܐ.

1) The only known copy of this letter is in the same Vatican MS. 107 (f. 60 r. to 63 v.) which furnishes us the various readings marked C for the letter of Jacob of Sarug. The copy seems to be very correct; unfortunately, the close is wanting.

IV.

LETTER OF MAR XENAIAS OF MABÛG

to Abraham and Orestes, presbyters of Edessa, concerning Stephen Bar Sudaili the Edessene.

I have learned that Stephen the scribe, who departed from among us some time since, and now resides in the country of Jerusalem, sent to you, some time ago, followers of his with letters and books composed by him; taking care at the same time that the arrival of those whom he had sent, as well as what he was astutely desirous of accomplishing, should be concealed from us. For he thought that, were I to learn that he had sent to you men and also writings, his hopes might be disappointed. He has insanely imagined — whence I know not, but certainly from Satan, for he is the Father and cause of every heresy — to put forth in a book an impious and foolish doctrine, which is worthy of being reputed not only a heresy, but worse than Heathenism and Judaism, because it openly assimilates the creation to God, and teaches that it is necessary for everything to become like him. It also falsifies the Holy Scriptures, and even destroys faith in Christianity, teaching that every man may sin as he pleases, and dissuading Heathen, Jews, and here-

ܘܫܟܠܠ ܐܦ ܠܗ̇ ܠܡܥܡܪܢܘܬܐ ܡܪܢܝܬܐ. ܘܠܡܗܝܡܢܘܬܐ
ܕܐܪ̈ܙܐ ܐܠܗ̈ܝܐ. ܘܠܡ̈ܠܟܐ ܘܠܪ̈ܘܚܐ ܕܥܠܡ ܕܙܗܝܪܘܬܐ. ܐ̱ܘ
ܒܪ ܐܝܟ ܡܠܬܗ ܪ̈ܒܘܬܐ ܠܗ ܒܠܚܘܕ ܕܝܠܗ ܠܗ ܐܝܬ:
ܐܠܐ ܐܦ ܠܚܕܐ ܡܢܝܘܬܐ ܕܦܘܪ̈ܕܝܐ ܒܠܚܘܕ ܡܬܬܚܝܕ.
ܘܚܕ ܐܝܬܘܗܝ، ܐܣܝܪܐ ܕܦܓܪܗ ܬܠܡܝܕܐ ܘܕܡܫܡܫܢ̱
ܫ̈ܢܐ. ܘܕܦܘܠܘܣ ܒܪܘܪܐ ܘܕܝܗܘܕܐ ܡܫܠܡܢܐ: ܘܕܫ̈ܠܝܚܐ
ܡܟܪ̈ܙܢܐ. ܗܘ̇ ܕܬܠܡܝܕܘܬ ܡܫܝܚܐ ܪܘܫܡܐ ܘܐܬܬܗ̇
ܕܦܪܘܬܐ: ܕܐܦ ܡܛܠ ܒܠܡܕܡ ܚܕ ܚܢܢܐ ܐܡܪ ܕܗܘܐ
ܡܢ ܐܠܗܐ. ܘܗܠܝܢ ܕܐܬܐܡ̈ܪܝ ܬܘܪ̈ܬܐ ܐܬܘܗܝ. ܘܠܚ̈ܒܪ
ܠܐ ܡܬ̈ܬܟܢܝܢ. ܘܫܪܝܪܐܝܬ ܒܓܠܐ ܫܠܝܚܐ ܘܬܠܡܝܕܘ ܠܟܠ
ܚܘ̈ܫܒܐ ܡܢ ܣܓܘܬܐ ܠܪܘܚܢܝܘܬܐ: ܐ̱ ܐܦ ܒܠܒܕ
ܬܘܠܡܕܐ ܘܡܥܡܪܢܘܬܐ ܒܬܪ ܦܝܣܟܐ ܐܝܘ̱ ܕܫܠܝܚܐ: ܘܚܕ
ܚܢܐ ܚܬܝܕܝܢ ܠܡܗܘܐ ܚܡ ܡܪܢܐ ܠܐ ܐܠܗܐ. ܘܠܐ ܡܚܠ
ܡܫܠܡܢ ܗܠܝܢ ܕܡܢܬܗ ܫܠܦ ܡܫܝܚܐ ܡܢ ܐܠܝܢ ܕܦܫܠܘ
ܐܢܘ̱. ܒܗ̇ ܕܠܐ ܐܝܠܝܢ ܕܐܣܘܪܘ ܡܕܡ ܬܘܪܐ ܢܡܣܝܢ.
ܘܠܐ ܗ̇ܢܘ̱ ܕܦܫܠܘ ܐܢܘ̱ ܒܡܕܡ ܢܡܘܣܝܢ. ܕܟܠܗܘ̱
ܐܚܝܕܐ ܐܝܟ ܕܐܡܪ ܠܘܬ ܚܕ ܫܘܡܠܝܐ ܡܬܬܡܟܢܝܢ. ܘܐܝܟ
ܗ̈ܕܡܐ ܕܒܓܘܫܡܐ ܕܐܝܬܝܗܘ̱ ܒܬܪ ܚܢܢܐ ܕܫܪܪܐ ܘܕܠܗ.
ܗܟܝܠ ܟܕ ܝܗܒܐ ܘܐܦ ܗ̣ܘ ܐܡܪ: ܕܗ̇ܘܝܢ ܒܐܠܗܐ ܘܒܡܫܚܗ
ܒܚܕܝܘܬܐ ܕܠܗܘܬ ܚܕ ܡܕܡ. ܘܡܬܝܕܥܝܢ ܗܠܝܢ ܐܝܟ ܕܐܡܪ:
ܒܐܪ̈ܙ ܚܕܡܢܐ ܕܗܘܐ ܒܗ ܐܝܟ ܡܠܬܗ ܐܠܗܐ ܟܠ ܒܟܠ.
ܚܕ ܚܢܢܐ. ܚܕܐ ܐܝܬܘܬܐ. ܚܕܐ ܐܠܗܘܬܐ. ܒܗ̇ ܕܐ̱
ܡܢܝܐ ܕܠܐܝܬܘܬܐ ܢܣܒܘ̱ ܒܬܪ ܐܢܫܐ ܒܬܪ ܚܕ ܚܢܢܐ:
ܡܕܒܪܢܘܬܐ ܕܒܦܓܪ ܘܡܬܒܪܢܝܢܘܬܐ ܡܢ ܬܘܪܐ ܗ̇ܘ. ܡܢ

tics from Christian instruction and from being converted to God. It makes of no effect holy Baptism, and the giving of the Divine mysteries, and labors and struggles for righteousness. For if, according to his impious words, not only will there be no Judgment, but all will receive the same measure of retribution, then the same honor will be accorded to the apostle Peter and to Simon Magus, to the preacher Paul and to the traitor Judas, to the Apostles and Evangelists [1]. And, what is especially full of an impiety akin to insanity is, that he says, that everything is of one nature with God. What has just been detailed is most important and most completely reprehensible; for then the Apostles have in vain worked, and converted all nations from Heathenism to Christianity, if even without instruction in the faith and baptism they are to be equals of the Apostles, and are to become consubstantial with God, the Lord of the Universe. Hence there is no difference between those who died for Christ and those who killed them, for they who were confessors of the faith will receive nothing more, and they who killed them nothing less, because all together, as he says, will arrive at one perfection; and as the members of the body are of the same nature as each other and as the body itself, so, as he means and even says, are we in God and with Him in unity the one with tho other. These things may be known, he says, by the mystery of the first day of the week, when, as he says, God will be all in all: one nature, one substance, one divinity. If then it is possible that men should become consubstantial with the Divinity, then the dispensation of the flesh and the Incarnation were superfluous. From misunderstanding, therefore,

---

1) The antithesis which must have followed seems to have been omitted in our copy.

ܠܐ ܡܫܬܡܗ ܒܪ ܕܠܝܬ ܡܠܬܐ ܗܝ ܕܡܫܝܚܐ ܕܢܗܘܐ ܐܠܗܐ
ܥܠ ܟܠ: ܒܪܐ ܘܪܒܒ ܡܠܟܐ ܗܢܐ ܪܫܝܐ ܘܡܫܠܛ.
ܐܝܟܐ ܕܐܡܪ ܐܦܠܐ ܥܠ ܬܫܥܐ ܐܬܦܠܓ. ܕܗܪܟܢ ܐܝܟ
ܕܦܪܨܘܦܐ ܐܦ ܠܡܫܡܫ ܗܝ ܕܒܬܪܟܢ ܠܡܗܘܐ ܒܪ ܐܠܗܐ
ܚܕ ܒܢܝܐ. ܡܛܠ ܕܐܦ ܒܠܫܘܢ ܐܝܟ ܕܟܠ ܫܘܠܛܢܐ
ܒܠܫܘܢ ܕܠܐ ܦܠܓ. ܐܡܪ ܕܒܬܪ ܚܕ ܒܢܝܐ ܒܬܪܟܢ ܠܡܗܘܐ
ܕܠܗ ܕܐܝܬܘܬܐ ܘܕܐܠܗܘܬܐ. ܘܥܠ ܕܠܐ ܒܗ ܒܡܠܬܐ
ܡܕܡ ܕܢܬܟܢ: ܘܠܐ ܒܡܠܝܢ ܕܡܫܡܫ ܕܢܒܘܪ: ܘܠܐ ܒܐܠܝܢ
ܕܐܡܪܢ ܥܠ ܒܬܪܐ: ܥܠ ܐܓܪܐ ܘܫܘܘܝܐ ܕܦܓܪܐ
ܘܒܬܪܐ ܚܙܝܢ ܕܢܬܟܢܐ. ܘܠܐ ܫܘܓܢܝܐ ܕܐܝܬ ܒܢܝܢܬ
ܐܝܬܘܬܐ ܠܒܪܝܬܐ ܡܢ ܠܡܫܝܚܗ: ܘܕܠܐ ܡܟܝܟܐ ܕܐܝܬܘܬܐ
ܒܪ ܫܘܠܛܢܐ ܒܪܝܬܐ ܬܗܘܐ: ܐܘ ܒܪܝܬܐ ܐܝܬܘܬܐ:
ܘܠܐ ܒܡܠܟܘܬܐ ܐܠܝܢ ܕܐܬܪܘܡܝܬ ܠܡܠܬܐ ܗܝ، ܦܫܘܩ ܦܠܓ:
ܢܓܕܐ ܕܒܪ ܡܬܚܫܘܢܐ ܐܝܟ ܡܫܘܚܐ ܘܫܘܡܪܢܐ. ܢܦܫܬ
ܐܦ ܗܘ ܡܪܡܣܘ ܒܡܕܝܢܬ ܢܘܚ ܡܪܢܐ: ܗܘ ܕܐܦ ܥܠܠ
ܘܟܠܐ ܢܦܩ ܀

ܐܫܟܚܬ ܕܝܢ ܒܡܫܡܫܢܘܬܗ. ܕܐܦ ܡܢ ܗܝ ܕܒܬܒܐ
ܒܐܘܓܠܝܘܢ ܕܐܡܪ ܡܪܢ: ܕܢܘܡܘܣܐ ܘܢܒܝܐ ܦܪܫ ܚܝܠܐ:»
ܘܢܘܡܘܣܐ ܕܐܠܗܐ ܡܬܚܬܠ. ܒܪܝܐ ܐܢܫܐ ܪܒܢ. ܒܗ
ܒܪܘܒܬܐ ܡܛܠ ܠܡܠܐ ܗܢܐ ܕܦܐܡ. ܘܡܪܝܗ ܐܦ ܒܢܝܐ.
ܘܠܥܒܕܬܐ ܠܢܦܫܬܐ ܕܐܡܪ ܕܗܘܝܐ ܒܬܪ ܫܘܠܡܐ. ܘܡܕܒܪܢܐ
ܐܡܪ ܕܐܝܬܘܗܝ ܫܘܡܠܝܐ ܕܒܗ ܒܬܪ ܕܢܗܘܐ ܐܠܗܐ
ܥܠ ܟܠ. ܗܘܘ ܕܝܢ ܕܟܠ ܡܕܡ ܗܘܐ ܒܐܠܗܐ. ܚܕ ܒܢܝܐ
ܘܚܕܐ ܐܝܬܘܬܐ. ܕܠܐ ܡܫܬܠ ܢܗܘܐ ܐܝܬ ܗܘ ܕܡܫܒܪ

this saying of the apostle, "that God may be all in all" [1]), he has foolishly imagined and produced this impious and foolish doctrine, which perhaps would not even be accepted among demons; for I think they would tremble simply to hear that they were to become consubstantial with God; for also concerning them, as well as all the angelic host which did not fall, does he assert, that they will become consubstantial with the Divinity and Godhead. And as he did not know how to understand this saying or to perceive what preceded it, neither was he able to consider all the things which are said in the Holy Scriptures on the reward of the righteous and the punishment of the wicked. Neither did he know how to distinguish between the Divinity and the creation, and that it is not possible for the Divinity through change to become the creation, or creation the Divinity. Furthermore he does not accord with the doctors who have interpreted this saying in an orthodox manner. He desired, being puffed up like a vain and proud man, to orginate heresies himself also, like John the Egyptian, whom for a short time he even followed.

I have also found in his writings that he has imagined another false doctrine, founded on what it is written in the Gospel that Our Lord said: "Today and tomorrow I work miracles, and on the third day I shall be perfected" [2]). He fancies that, speaking in a parable, this world was established on the sixth day of the week, and he calls it evil; and the Sabbath (he calls) the rest which comes after the completion; and the first day of the week, he says, is the consummation, because then God will become all in all; that is, everything will be in God, one nature and one substance; so

1) I Corinth. XV, 28.
2) Luke XIII, 32. It is differently quoted later: see p. 37.

ܘܗܢܘܢ ܕܡܦܠܚܝܢ ܡܕܒܪܢܘܬܗ: ܘܕܝܪ̈ܐ ܟܐܠܝܢ ܕܒܗܘܢ
ܡܬܝܕܥܐ. ܘܠܐ ܗܘܐ ܐܒܐ ܘܒܪܐ ܘܪܘܚܐ ܬܠܝܬܝܘܬܗܘܢ.
ܡܢ ܚܕ ܡܫܠܡܝܢ ܒܠܗ ܕܗܘܢܐ ܘܡܟܬܒܐ ܚܒܘܫܐ ܚܢܢ ܐܢ
ܚܕ: ܚܕ ܚܝܠܐ ܘܡܠܘܟܐ ܒܪܒܘ ܕܗܘܝܢ. ܐܡܝܢܐ ܡܫܒ̈ܚܐ
ܒܬܪ ܚܕ ܚܝܠܐ: *ܠܐ ܡܢ ܡܬܪܐ ܢܦܩܘܢ ܐܦ ܗܢܘܢ ܚܕ
ܡܫܘܚܬܐ: ܘܢܗܘܐ ܡܚܝܠ ܒܥܠܡܐ. ܠܐ ܒܠܚܘܕ ܕܒܪܝܬܐ
ܒܗ ܐܝܬܘܬܐ. ܐܠܐ ܘܕܠܗܘܢ ܕܡܫܒ̈ܚܐ ܚܕ ܒܗ ܚܕ.
ܒܚܕ ܕܝܢ ܕܐܡܪ ܕܗܠܝܢ ܠܗ ܒܠܚܘܕ ܬܠܬܐ ܩ̈ܢܘܡܝܢ ܒܪܘܟܬܐ
ܘܥܒܕܬܐ ܘܫܘܒܚܐ: ܐܝܬܝܗܘܢ ܬܪ̈ܝܢ ܘܦܪ̈ܨܘܦܐ ܘܩ̈ܠܐ ܬܢܝܐ.
ܠܗܠܝܢ ܚܕܐ ܠܒܪ ܡܢ. ܐܘ ܚܢܢ ܒܠܚܘܕ ܐܠܗܝܐ ܕܡܫܬܒܪܘܢ
ܕܐܝܬܝܗܘܢ ܗܒܝܠܐ. ܐܘ ܕܐܦܠܐ ܗܠܝܢ ܡܬܝܕܥܝܢ ܐܝܟ
ܕܗܘܐ ܐܡܪ. ܒܚܕ ܕܝܢ ܐܝܠ ܒܬܪ ܡܫܠܡܢܘܬܐ ܡܫܘܕܥܬܐ.
ܬܘܒ ܐܦ ܡܢ ܒܬܪ ܡܢܝܬܐ ܬܪ̈ܝܢ ܦܘܪ̈ܫܢܐ. ܘܠܚܕ ܦܬܪܐ
ܢܫܬܐ ܘܠܐܚܪܢܐ ܥܘܡܠܢܐ. ܠܚܕ ܫܪܝܪܘܬܐ ܘܠܚܪܢܐ (sic)
ܐܠܗܘܬܐ. ܒܡ ܥܒ̈ܕܗܐ ܐܚܪ̈ܢܐ ܕܡܬܠܬܠܗܘܢ ܕܗܠܝܢ ܦܬܐ
ܘܗܡ. ܠܒܘܕܐ ܚܢܢ ܒܠܚܘܕ ܗܘܬ ܗܕܐ ܡܪܝܫܝܬܐ: ܘܐܡܪܘ
ܕܡܢ ܒܬܪ ܡܢܝܬܐ ܗܘܐ ܢܫܬܐ ܐܠܦ ܥܢ̈ܝ. ܘܕܪ̈ܝܫܐ
ܐܦܠܝܢ ܘܦܘܡܝܢ. ܘܣܦܪ̈ܐ ܦܘܢܝܢ ܘܡܬܦܪܫܝܢ. ܘܡܐܢ̈ܐ
ܡܬܦܪܦܝܢ ܒܟܠ ܢܫܡܐ ܦܪܘܫܐ. ܘܦܬ̈ܠܐ ܡܫܒܚܝܢ ܒܠ
ܥܘܢܝܢ. ܕܠܗܘܬ ܡܫܒܚܢܘܬܐ ܗܕܐ ܒܬܪ ܕܐܡܪ ܡܢ
ܕܦܠܝܢ ܐܝܬܘܢ ܕܠܐ ܡܕܡ ܐܝܬܘܢ ܒ̈ܬܠܐ ܘܠܐ ܚܠܡ»
ܕܐܠܗܐ. ܕܒܫܡܝܬܐ ܕܡܬܬܐ ܠܐ ܐܦܠܝܢ ܘܠܐ ܥܒܝܡ ܘܠܐ»
ܡܬܕܘܟܢ. ܐܠܐ ܐܝܬܝܗܘܢ ܐܝܟ ܬܠܐܟܐ ܕܐܠܗܐ». ܘܐܢ
ܕܝܢ ܠܗܝ ܕܐܡܒܪ ܕܐܫܬܪܬܐ ܗܝ ܢܫܬܐ ܘܐܫܬܪܬܐ ܗܝ

that there will no longer be, He who creates and those who receive his creative action; He who shows benevolence to those whom He loves; and there will no longer be Father, Son and Spirit; for, if he raves that the Creator and all his creatures who are distinct from each other will become one nature and person, how must not consubstantial persons of necessity also become one person? Thus there would be a confusion, not only of the creation with the Divine Substance, but also of the Persons one with another.

But in that he says that these three days alone, the sixth, seventh and first days of the week are mysteries, types and parables, he has posited this alternative: it is necessary either to believe that all (the days) are to receive this manner of interpretation, or else not to believe that those are as he says.

Following the Jewish doctrine, he appoints after the resurrection two retributions, one of which he calls *rest* [1]) and the other *perfection*, one *liberty* and the other *divinity*, together with other names which he has contrived and applied to them. For to the Jews alone had this theory occurred, who say that after the resurrection there will be a rest of a thousand years, during which the righteous will eat and drink, and sinners will hunger and thirst; the just will give themselves up to every bodily delight, and the wicked will suffer every torment. Concerning which belief it is written that Our Lord said: "Ye do err, not knowing the Scriptures nor the power of God: for in the resurrection of the dead they do not eat nor drink, neither marry, but are as the angels of God" [2]). But regarding his belief, that *rest* is one thing and the *kingdom* another; and the glory

1) Cf. Hebrews III and IV.

2) Matth. XXII, 29—30 and Mark XII, 24—25; the eating and drinking is an interpolation.

ܡܠܟܘܬܐ: ܘܐܘܪܚܐ ܫܘܡܫܐ ܕܗܕܝܢ ܫܘܡܠܝܐ: ܘܐܘܪܚܐ
ܗܘ ܫܘܡܠܝܐ. ܢܐܡܪ ܡܢ ܐܢܫܐ ܕܠܒܐ ܘܕܝܫܐ ܐܘ ܢܟܝܐ
ܐܘ ܫܠܝܚܐ ܐܘ ܡܠܐܟܐ ܦܬܠ: ܘܕܠܡܐ ܬܠܬ ܬܠܬܐ ܠܦܣܩܐ
ܦܠܓ. ܐܫܬܟܠ ܒܪ ܐܝܟ ܕܐܡܪ. ܠܒܪܘܟܬܐ ܡܬܐܒܘܬܐ.
ܒܝ ܢܡܣܟ ܠܒܣܡܐ ܕܡܬܐܒܘܬܐ ܡܢ ܣܓܝܐܐ ܐܘܟܪܣ.
ܘܠܒܬܐ ܗܝ ܕܒܠ ܘܟܠܗ ܡܣܝܐ. ܘܠܣܓܒܝܐ ܗܝ ܕܢܗܘܐ
ܐܠܗܐ ܟܠ ܒܟܠ. ܘܗܘ ܕܒܬܪܐ ܗܕܐ ܕܠܬܚܬ ܐܢܫ
ܠܡܫܝܚܐ: ܡܢ ܗܝ ܕܢܗܘܐ ܒܐܠܗܐ. ܘܟܠ ܗܠܝܢ ܬܠܬ ܬܠܬ ܡܦܪ
ܕܡܦܩܢ. ܡܢ ܡ̈ܠܐ ܕܐܡܪ ܡܪܢ ܠܘܬ ܦ̈ܪܝܫܐ. ܐܝܠܝܢ ܕܕܝܢܐ
ܕܠܐ ܠܦܘܩܕܢܐ ܘܠܐ ܦܠܚܘܬܐ ܘܠܐ ܡܬܠܐ ܘܠܐ ܐܘܪܚܐ.
ܐܠܐ ܬܫܒܘܚܬܐ ܕܡܫܒܚܢܐ ܕܡܫܝܚܘܬܗ ܕܦ̈ܪܝܫܐ ܐܬܪܒܒ.
ܐܝܟ ܡܐ ܕܡܘܕܥ ܗܘ ܦܘܠܘܣ. ܒܗ ܠܡ ܒܗܘ ܡܫܡܥܐ.»
ܦܪܘܫ ܐܢܫܐ ܡܢ ܦ̈ܪܝܫܐ ܘܐܡܪܝܢ ܠܗ. ܦܘܩ ܙܠ ܡܟܐ.»
ܡܛܠ ܕܗܪܘܕܣ ܨܒܐ ܕܢܩܛܠܟ. ܘܐܡܪ ܠܗܘܢ. ܙܠܘ ܐܡܪܘ»
ܠܬܥܠܐ ܗܢܐ. ܕܗܐ ܡܦܩ ܐܢܐ ܫ̈ܐܕܐ. ܘܐܣܝܘܬܐ ܓܡܪ»
ܐܢܐ ܝܘܡܢܐ ܘܡܚܪ ܘܠܝܘܡܐ ܕܬܠܬܐ ܡܫܬܡܠܐ ܐܢܐ.»
ܒܪܡ ܘܠܐ ܠܝ ܕܝܘܡܢܐ ܘܡܚܪ ܐܗܠܟ. ܘܠܗܘ ܕܒܬܪܗ»
ܐܙܠ. ܡܛܠ ܕܠܐ ܡܫܟܚܐ ܕܢܐܒܕ ܢܒܝܐ ܠܒܪ ܡܢ ܐܘܪܫܠܡ.»
ܘܐܦ ܐܝܟ ܡܪܢܝܬܐ ܕܗܘ ܝܘܡܢܐ ܒܪܘܟܬܐ ܦܠܐܬܐ ܗܝ
ܕܗܢܐ ܥܠܡܐ: ܘܡܚܪ ܫܒܬܐ ܠܦܘܣܐ ܕܢܝܚܬܐ. ܘܠܣܓܒܝܐ
ܝܘܡܢܐ ܕܬܠܬܐ ܐܘܪܐ ܕܫܘܡܠܝܐ. ܡܕܝܢ ܡܢ ܒܬܪ ܫܘܡܠܝܐ:
ܬܘܒ ܒܬܪ ܡܢ ܕܢܓܠܐ. ܐܘܪܐ ܘܡܢ ܡܢܗ. ܕܗܢܐ ܐܦ
ܡܦܪܫܐ ܐܝܟ ܡܠܬܗ ܕܦܘܠܘܣ ܠܗܘܢ ܚܕ ܒܢܝܐ ܒܢ ܐܠܗܐ.
ܗܒܢܐ ܒܪ ܒܬܪܟܐ ܕܐܡܪ ܡܪܢ ܡܢ ܒܬܪ ܗܝ ܕܝܘܡܢܐ»

before the consummation one thing, and the *consummation* itself another; we would ask, from what Holy Book, or prophet, or apostle, or teacher, has he received this doctrine of a division into three orders? For he understands, as he says, by the sixth day *motion*, having taken the term *motion* from the monk Evagrius [1]); by the Sabbath, that Christ will be all and in all men; and by the first day, that God will be all in all. He furthermore shows that it is less for man to be united to Christ than to be in God. He imagined, then, that he could confirm these three (stages) by the words which Our Lord spoke to the Pharisees, which it is certain were not a figure, an allegory, a parable, or a mystery, but the narration of an action imagined by the Pharisees, as is shown by reading them. "The same day there came certain of the Pharisees, saying unto him, Get thee out and depart hence, for Herod desireth to kill thee. And He said unto them, Go ye, and tell that fox, Behold I cast out devils and I perform cures today and tomorrow, and the third day I shall be perfected. Nevertheless I must *work* [2]) today and tomorrow, and on the day following I will go (hence) [3]), for it cannot be that a Prophet perish out of Jerusalem" [4]). Now if, according to his researches, today, the sixth day, be an allegory of this world, and tomorrow, the Sabbath, a type of rest, and the third day, the first of the week, a symbol of the consummation; what then comes after the consummation? Is Our Lord again to be crucified? but by whom? for according to his doctrine even the Jews will have become of one nature with God.

Now it is thus written, that Our Lord said, after "today

1) Κίνησις. Evagrius Ponticus was a disciple of Gregory Nazianzen.

2) The expression *work* instead of *walk* is in the Peshitta, but not in the Curetonian Gospels.

3) The Curetonian version reads ܘܒܬܪ ܡܚܪ ܐܙܠܢܐ.

4) Luke XIII, 31—33.

ܘܡܚܘܐ ܘܠܫܘܡܠܝܐ ܕܬܠܝܬܝܘܬܐ ܡܫܬܡܠܝܐ ܐܝܬܝܗ. ܡܛܠ ܕܠܐ«
ܠܡ ܡܫܟܚܐ ܕܢܒܝܐ ܢܐܒܕ ܠܒܪ ܡܢ ܐܘܪܫܠܡ». ܒܗ̇ ܫܘܡܠܝܐ
ܕܝܢܐ ܕܦܪܐ ܠܗ̇ ܕܡܬܓܠܠ. ܘܗܕܐ ܡܫܬܒܪܐ ܒܐܘܪܫܠܡ.
ܐܝܟܢܐ ܕܐܦ ܢܒܝ̈ܐ ܟܠܗܘܢ ܐܬܢܒܝܘ. ܘܐܟܘܬܗܘܢ ܘܐܦ
ܗ̇ܘ ܟܬܒܐ ܕܟܬ̇ܒ ܢܬܓܠܠ. ܘܐܡܪ ܕܒܗ̇ ܨܠܝܒܐ ܡܫܬܡܠܝܐ.
ܥܠ ܕܢܫܬܡܠܐ ܠܗ̇ ܕܐܡܪ ܒܗ ܒܨܠܝܒܐ ܕܗܘܐ ܫܠܡ. ܘܥܠ
ܗ̇ܝ ܐܘܪܚܬܐ ܕܐܬܬ ܥܒܬܐ ܕܢܥܬܒܕ ܒܪܗ ܕܐܠܗܐ».
ܘܥܠ ܗ̇ܝ ܕܡܟܐ ܕܬܬܪܫܡܫܢ ܠܒܪܗ ܕܐܠܗܐ: ܗܕܝܢ«
ܬ̇ܕܥܘܢ ܕܐܠܗܐ ܐܢܐ. ܘܡܕܡ ܡܢ ܨܒܘܬ ܢܦܫܝ ܠܐ«
ܒܥܒܕܢܐ». ܦܬ̈ܓܡܐ ܕܝܢ ܗܠܝܢ ܕܦܩܕܢ ܗܘܘ ܒܫܡܫܬܐ
ܕܢܝܢ ܗܘܘ ܕܟܠܗ ܡܢ̈ܝ: ܘܫܪܝ ܐܬ̈ܬܐ ܘܡܫܬܒܚ ܡܢ
ܟܠܢ: ܨܒܐ ܕܢܫܡܫܘܢ ܡܢ ܠܘܬܗܘܢ ܠܕܘܟܬܐ ܐܚܪܬܐ
ܕܠܐ ܗܟܢ ܢܬܚܫܒܘܢ. ܒܗ̇ ܕܝܢ ܬܫܒܘܚܬܐ ܕܡܢ ܟܠܢܫ
ܡܬܚܫܒܐ ܠܗ: ܘܒܗ̇ ܦܪܩܝܢ ܕܡܪܗܘܢ ܐܘ ܡܒܣܠܝܢ ܠܗ.
ܐܡܪܘ ܕܦܘܩ ܙܠ ܠܟ ܡܟܐ ܕܗܪܘܕܣ ܨܒܐ ܠܡܩܛܠܟ».
ܗ̣ܘ ܕܝܢ ܠܗܘܢ ܐܡܪ. ܕܠܒܪ ܡܢ ܨܒܝܢܗ ܠܐ ܡܫܟܚܐ.
ܘܠܐ ܗܪܘܕܣ ܘܠܐ ܗܢܘܢ: ܠܒܪ ܡܢ ܐܒܐ ܕܗ̣ܘ ܫܕܪܗ
ܡܫܡܫܝܢ ܦܩܕܝܢ ܠܗ. ܘܥܠ ܗܕܐ ܒܗ̇ ܫܪܝ ܒܗܪܘܕܣ ܘܐܡܪ
ܬܥܠܐ. ܗ̇ܘ ܕܫܠܝܛܐ ܗܘ ܒܠܚܘܕ ܘܡܫܠܛܢܐ. ܘܠܗ ܕܢܩܛܠ
ܡܕܡ ܒܝܫܐ ܕܗܘܐ ܚܫܒ ܠܗ ܕܢܥܒܕ ܠܐ ܡܫܟܚ. ܘܠܐ ܠܡ«
ܐܡܪܘ ܠܬܥܠܐ ܗܢܐ. ܕܗܐ ܡܦܩ ܐܢܐ ܫ̈ܐܕܐ. ܘܡܥܒܕ«
ܐܢܐ ܐܣܘ̈ܬܐ ܣܥܪ ܐܢܐ ܝܘܡܢܐ ܘܡܚܪ. ܘܠܝܘܡܐ ܕܬܠܬܐ ܡܫܬܡܠܐ«
ܐܢܐ». ܒܗ̇ ܪܡܙ ܥܠ ܫ̈ܢܝܐ ܬܠܬ ܗܠܝܢ ܕܐܬܬܗܦܟ ܒܝܢܬ
ܝܗܘ̈ܕܝܐ ܡܢ ܡܥܡܘܕܝܬܗ ܘܥܕܡܐ ܠܨܠܝܒܐ. ܕܒܗ̇ ܐܦ
ܐܠܦ ܕܡܚܪ ܬܕܡܘܪ̈ܬܐ ܡܛܠ ܕܒܗܠܝܢ ܫ̈ܢܝܐ ܬܠܬܝܢ ܕܥܒܕ

and tomorrow and the third day I shall be perfected", "because it cannot be that a prophet perish out of Jerusalem": it is therefore evident that He means, by the consummation, that He should be crucified, and that this should take place in Jerusalem, where also all the prophets had been killed, and likewise He also was to be crucified there. He said that He would be perfected through the cross, in order to fulfil what is said: "By the cross which consummates" [1]); and this other: "The hour is come that the Son of Man should be glorified" [2]), and also: „When ye have lifted up the Son of Man, then shall ye know that I do nothing of myself" [3]). Now the Pharisees, burning with envy because they saw that Our Lord taught and performed miracles and was glorified of all men, wished to expel him from among them unto some other place, that they should not be thus vexed. But, as praise from all men was given to him, they thought to intimidate and terrify him, and said: "Get thee out and depart hence, for Herod desireth to kill thee". But He said unto them that except He were willing He would not die, and that neither Herod nor they would be able to kill him except at the time He chose. Therefore, when He derides Herod and calls him fox, He indicates that he is but contemptible and despicable, and unable to kill Him before the time at which He has determined to die: "Go ye and tell that fox, Behold I cast out devils and perform cures today and tomorrow, and the third day I shall be perfected". He hereby indicates the three years which He passed among the Jews, from His baptism to His crucifixion, in which He also teaches that He worked miracles; for in the thirty years which preceded

1) There seems to be no such expression in Scripture.
2) John XII, 23.
3) From John VIII, 28.

ܡܥܡܘܕܝܘܬܐ. ܠܐ ܡܠܦܢܘܬܐ ܒܠܚܘܕ ܕܐܦܪܝܢ. ܘܠܐ ܐܬܐ
ܩܕܡ ܫܘܝ. ܐܠܐ ܐܡܪ ܕܗܢ ܒܬܪ ܬܠܬ ܫܢܝܢ ܕܐܬܬܣܝܡ
ܘܡܢܝܢܐ ܘܡܢܝܢ ܘܫܘܡܥܐ ܕܬܠܬܐ. ܒܝܘܡܐ ܕܗܘ ܟܕ ܐܙܠ
ܠܐܘܪܫܠܡ. ܘܬܡܢ ܡܬܛܠܠ ܡܢ ܫܘܕܥܐ: ܕܠܐ ܡܫܟܚܐ
ܕܢܒܝܐ ܢܐܒܕ ܠܒܪ ܡܢ ܐܘܪܫܠܡ. ܘܟܠ ܗܕܐ ܐܡܪ.
«ܕܐܘܪܫܠܡ ܠܡ ܐܘܪܫܠܡ. ܩܛܠܬ ܢܒܝܐ ܘܪܓܡܬ ܠܐܝܠܝܢ
«ܕܫܠܝܚܝܢ ܠܘܬܗ. ܟܡܐ ܙܒܢܝܢ ܨܒܝܬ ܠܡܟܢܫܘ ܒܢܝܟܝ:
«ܐܝܟܢܐ ܕܬܪܢܓܠܬܐ ܟܢܫܐ ܦܪܘܓܝܗ ܬܚܝܬ ܓܦܝܗ. ܘܠܐ
«ܨܒܝܬܘܢ. ܗܐ ܡܫܬܒܩ ܠܟܘܢ ܒܝܬܟܘܢ ܚܪܒܐ. ܐܡܪܢܐ
«ܠܟܘܢ ܕܝܢ ܕܠܐ ܬܚܙܘܢܢܝ ܥܕܡܐ ܕܬܐܬܐ [ܝܘ]ܡܐ ܕܬܐܡܪܘܢ:
ܒܪܝܟ ܗܘ ܕܐܬܐ ܒܫܡܗ ܕܡܪܝܐ». ܐܦ ܐܢܬ ܗܟܝܠ ܒܗܠܝܢ
ܕܐܬܡܪܝ: ܐܘ ܬܫܘܒܚܬܐ ܐܘ ܦܓܘܥܐ: ܐܘ ܡܕܡ ܕܠܐܝܬܘܗܝ
ܐܘ ܙܒܢܝܢܐܝܬ ܡܘܕܐ ܒܐܝܠܝܢ ܕܠܗܘܢ ܐܬܝܢ. ܦܪܘ ܐܢܬܘܢ
ܘܐܬܡܠܟܘ. ܘܫܡܥܘ ܚܡܫܘܢ ܐܦ ܠܫܪܪܐ. ܡܛܠ ܕܟܠܗ
ܗܠܝܢ ܬܠܬ ܬܠܬܐ ܡܢܝܢܝܢ ܐܝܟ ܕܩܕܡ ܠܬܪܝܢܘܬܗ ܦܪܘܫܘܬܐ:
ܘܠܦܘܫܩܐ ܕܪܘܚܢܐ ܬܠܬܐ ܕܒܪܘܚܬܐ ܘܕܡܫܒܚܬܐ ܘܕܩܕܝܫܘܬܐ.
ܘܡܢܝܢܐ ܠܡ ܐܡܪ ܘܡܢܝܢ ܕܐܬܬܘܗܝ ܒܠܚܘܕܝܐ ܒܢܝܐ
ܘܫܪܘܬܐ. ܘܗܝ ܕܡܬܡܠܝܐ ܠܡܢܝܢܐ ܕܬܠܬܐ. ܗܝ ܕܡܢܝܢܐ
ܐܠܗܝܐ ܥܠ ܟܠ. ܘܗܝ ܕܡܢܝܢܐ ܒܠܚܘܕ ܒܡܫܝܚܐ ܒܪܗ
ܫܠܡܬܐ. ܐܝܟ ܗܘ ܕܡܒܥܠ ܠܗ ܗܘܝܢ ܒܪܗ ܡܥܡܘܕܝܘܬܐ:
ܗܟܢ ܕܡܢܝܢܐ ܗܝ ܕܒܠ ܘܡܠܘܢ ܡܫܝܚܐ. ܕܐܢ ܗܘܐ
ܒܫܠܡܐ ܗܘܝܐ. ܡܢܝܢ ܒܪܘܚܬܐ ܘܠܐ ܡܕܡ ܗܘܝܐ. ܘܠܐ
ܐܬܒܪܝܢ ܘܐܬܬܠܝ ܡܫܝܚܐ. ܘܠܐ ܫܢ ܘܡܟܬ. ܘܠܐ ܐܫܬܪܝ
ܫܘܠܛܢܗ ܕܡܘܬܐ ܘܐܘܫܪܢܗ ܕܫܝܠܐ. ܘܠܝܢ ܠܒܪ ܘܕܐܝܢ

His baptism it is not written that He gave any instruction or manifested any miracle. But He says that after three years, which are today, tomorrow and the third day, at the time that He chooses He will go up to Jerusalem, and there will be crucified by the Jews, "for it cannot be that a prophet perish out of Jerusalem". And to this He adds: "O Jerusalem, Jerusalem, that killest the prophets and stonest them which are sent unto thee; how often would I have gathered thy children together as a hen doth gather her chickens under her wings, and ye would not! Behold your house is left unto you desolate. For I say unto you, Ye shall not see me until the day come when ye shall say, Blessed is he that cometh in the name of the Lord" [1]).

Therefore, whether or no there be in these words a symbol or type or anything which allegorically and mystically teaches the things which appear unto this man, read ye and consider and decide among yourselves: for by these three words he sustains, as he imagines, his vain opinion, and the change of the three dispensations of the sixth, the seventh and the first days of the week. For he calls today and tomorrow (respectively) the evil world and liberty, and the being perfected on the third day is, that God will be all in all. All being in Christ on the seventh day (Sabbath) — as if they were not so already by baptism — he believes to indicate that Christ *is* all and *in* all men. If this be on the seventh day then nothing took place on the sixth, and Christ was not made flesh and born, and did not suffer and die, neither was the power of death and the reign of corruption destroyed.

1) Matthew XXIII, 37—39; Luke XIII, 34—35. ܕܢܐܬܐ ܝܘܡܐ, "the day come", is not found in the Peshitta, but in the Curetonian version: otherwise the Peshitta for Luke XIII is followed except ܐܝܟܢܐ ܕ = ܐܝܟ and ܒܫܡܐ for ܕܒܫܡܐ; ܐܡܿܪܢܐ = ܐܡܪ ܐܢܐ; ܕܗܐ = ܗܐ.

ܗܠܝܢ ܒܗ̇ ܨܠܝܒܐ ܘܡܘܬܐ ܕܡܫܝܚܐ ܗ̇ܘ. ܕܗܘܐ ܒܥܪܘܒܬܐ
ܐܣܬܒܪ. ܐܝܟܢܐ ܕܐܦ ܡܟܐ ܘܐܡܪ. ܕܗܘܐ ܟܠ ܡܕܡ
ܐܫܬܠܡ. ܗܕܐ ܕܝܢ ܗܢܐ ܐܬܦܪܫܬ ܒܠܚܘܕ ܒܝܘܡܐ. ܐܘ
ܡܢ ܒܥܪܘܒܬܐ ܐܠܦ ܕܗܘܬ ܫܘܡܠܝܐ: ܒܗ̇ ܗ̇ܝ ܕܗܘܐ
ܟܠ ܡܕܡ ܡܫܠܡ: ܗ̇ܘ ܕܝܢ ܠܫܒܬܐ ܠܗܕܐ ܦܪܫ.
ܚܠܝܐܝܬ ܠܗܘܢ ܡܠܬܐ ܕܦܘܩ ܐܣܬܟܠ. ܡܢ ܗܟܝܠ
ܒܥܪܘܒܬܐ ܚܕ ܘܡܛܠ. ܘܫܕܐ ܫܘܠܛܢܐ ܕܫܢ̈ܐ ܘܕܡܘܬܐ.
ܘܫܒܬܐ ܗܘܐ ܟܠܗ ܡܪܝܐ. ܘܐܒܒܪ ܒܡ ܕܗܠܝܢ ܐܦ ܫܘܠܛܢܐ
ܕܫܢܐ. ܘܗܟܢ ܐܦ ܠܢܦܫܬܐ ܗܠܝܢ ܕܐܬܝܗ̈ܒ ܗܘ̈ܝ ܟܠܗ
ܫܘܠ. ܘܫܒܬܒܬܐ ܗܘ ܡܢ ܒܬ ܡܝܬܐ. ܘܗܘ ܒܗ̇ ܕܠܗ
ܡܫܘܬܐ ܕܟܠܢܫ. ܘܫܘܪܝܐ ܕܟܠܗܝܢ ܫܢ̈ܬܐ ܗ̇ܘ ܕܠܝܬ ܒܗ
ܫܢܬܐ ܘܫܒܥܬܐ ܐܝܟ ܕܗܘܐ ܐܡܪ. ܐܠܐ ܫܒܥܬܐ ܟܠܗ.
ܒܗܠܝܢ ܗܟܝܠ ܒܗ̇ ܠܐ ܚܕ ܗܘܐ ܠܡܣܪ: ܘܠܐ ܕܡܐܠܦ
ܙܒܢܐ ܡܢ ܗ̇ܢܘܢ ܕܐܬܡܒܝܢ. ܗܘܘܬ (?) ܗ̇ܘ ܠܗ ܦܦܪܐ. ܘܠܦ
ܡܢ ܫܘܫܒܗܘܢ ܗܬܝܡܐ. ܘܠܐ ܡܢ ܟܬ̈ܒܐ ܩ̈ܕܝܫܐ. ܘܪܒܒ
ܘܠܦܝܐ ܫܢܬܐ ܕܟܠܐ ܗܫܠܘܬܐ ܘܪܘܫܡܐ ܒܗ̇ ܡܬܠܠܐ
ܒܫܘܡܐ ܘܫܠܦܘܪܐ. ܗ̇ܘ ܒܝܢ ܕܐܦܠܐ ܡܠܬܐ ܕܫܘܝܐ
ܠܗܘܢܐ ܒܕܒܠ ܐܬܚܙܝ ܕܢܬܚܘܝ. ܒܗ̇ ܡܬܚܘܝܐ ܡܫܬܘܝܐ
ܕܗܪ̈ܦܘܫ ܢܦܫܗ ܗܘ. ܠܐ ܒܪ ܐܢܫ ܐܦܠܐ ܗܕܐ. ܒܗ̇
ܠܒ ܫܒܥܐ ܡܫܘܗܝ ܕܦܘܬܚܗܘܢ. ܕܐܝܬܘ ܠܗܘܢ ܐܬܢ̈ܝܐ
ܥܢ̈ܝܐ ܘܐܡܪܘ. ܕܟܠܗ ܠܡܠܬܗ ܘܐܫܟܚܘ ܕܟܬܝܒ ܠܗ ܟܠ
ܐܦܘܬܐ. ܕܟܠ ܒܝ ܒܪ ܚܝܒܐ ܗܘ ܕܐܬܬܘܬܐ. ܘܗܝ ܕܒܕܠܘܗ̇
ܦܪ ܠܡܘܕܥܐ: ܘܐܬܝܚܕ ܠܫܘܢܐ ܡܫܬ̈ܢܝܐ ܘܪܦܛܘ. ܕܫܠ
ܘܪܘܚܗܘܢ ܡܢ ܐܦܘܬܐ. ܘܫܒܗܘܢ ܡܫܒܚܐܝܬ ܒܒܘ̈ܬܐ ∻

For these and like things were accomplished by the crucifixion and death of Christ, which took place on the sixth day; who also cried out and said: "All is finished". This is what this man calls the evil world. Furthermore, as Our Lord taught that the consummation was on the sixth day, because He then fulfilled all things, this man by defining it to be on the first day of the week openly teaches contrary to the word of Our Lord. Our Lord therefore on the sixth day suffered and died and destroyed the dominion of suffering and of death; on the seventh day He was in the grave, and put an end also to the power of corruption, and visited the souls held captive in Sheol. And on the first day of the week He rose from the dead, and proved by His own resurrection that of all mankind, and the beginning of a new world in which there is no seventh and first day of the week, as this man says, but it is all first day. But he (Bar Sudaili) not being able to see these things himself, nor willing to learn them from those who were able, wrote this book in which he consulted his own vain thoughts and not the Holy Scriptures, and constructed a new doctrine full of wickedness and impiety, in an insipid and foolish language. For although he is not even able to command a language worthy of writing, still, being desirous of making a display, he came forward as an inventor of heresies. I will not, furthermore, omit the following fact, although it is apparent from his writings. There came unto me trustworthy men who said that on entering his cell they found written by him on the wall: "All nature is consubstantial with the Divine Essence"; and on account of their strongly accusing him of blasphemy, and it becoming known to many monks who murmured at it, he was afraid and removed it from the wall; but secretly put it into his writings.

ܠܫܐ. ܕܝܢ ܡܢ ܡܫܘ̈ܕܥܢܐ ܕܐܫܬܘܕܥ ܠܘܬ ܡܕܪܐ ܕܐܟܣܢܝܘܬܐ
ܗܠܝܢ ܕܒܝܬ ܐܒܪܗܡ. ܟܕ ܐܙܠ ܘܩܒܠ ܠܘܬܗ. ܗܕܐ ܡܠܬܐ
ܬܘܒ ܡܕܡ ܕܐܡܪ ܠܗ. ܠܐ ܬܕܚܠ. ܘܠܐ ܬܒܥܐ ܠܝ: ܟܠ
ܕܡܬܐܡܪܬ ܘܡܘܦܩܐ. ܕܫܠܡܝܢ ܒܗ ܐܒܪܗܡ ܐܝܬܘܗܝ ܚܠܦ
ܕܐܡܪ ܠܗ ܡܪܢ: ܕܐܝܠܝܢ ܕܝܢ ܐܟܣܢܝ̈ܐ ܠܕ̈ܝܪܐ ܡܫܠܡܢܘܬ
ܦܓܪ ܘܗܠܠ. ܐܦ ܐܟܣܢܝ̈ܐ ܐܢܫ̈ܐ ܕܕܪܫܘ ܒܒܝܬܗ ܡܛܠ ܗܢܐ
ܥܪܒܐ ܕܗܘܘ ܒܒܝܬܗ ܘܟܢܫܐ ܦܚܝܠܬܐ: ܐܝܠܝܢ ܕܗܘܫܐ
ܐܬܚܣܢܘ ܒܒܘܪܐ ܕܐܠܦܘܟܢܐ. ܐܡܪܘ ܡܕܡ ܗܘ̣ ܕܡܛܠ
ܥܢܪܬܘܗܝ ܦܘܠܚܢܬܐ ܕܕ̈ܝܪܐ. ܠܐ ܐܬܚܝܣ، ܠܝ ܕܦܠܚܐ
ܕܢܬܚܫܒܘܢ ܒܐܓܪܬܐ. ܐ̱ ܗܟܝܠ ܚܝܒ ܠܗܬܒܘܢ ܐܝܟ
ܕܠܦܬ: ܐܘ ܕܫܪܪ ܠܒܗܘܢ ܬܘܒܐ ܕܬܘܕܝܬܗܘܢ؛ ܚܙܘ ܕܗܠܝܢ
ܠܐܚܝ ܠܐ ܢܬܚܫܒܘܢ. ܘܢܬܪܐܣ ܠܗܠܝܢ ܕܝܩܝ̈ܪܬܐ ܕܒܬ̈ܒܝܢ
ܒܒܢܝܐ ܕܒܕܬܐ. ܕܠܐ ܡܢ ܟܠܗ ܦܫܝܛܘܬܐ ܘܪܦܝܘܬܐ:
ܗܠܝܢ ܕܡܢ ܟܝܢܐ ܥܒܝܕܝܢ ܠܢܫ̈ܐ ܢܫ̈ܝܟܝ. ܦܠܐ ܟܒܪ ܠܟܠ
ܢܘܟܪܝܐ ܕܐܝܟ ܡܢܐ ܕܥܒܕ ܠܗ. ܢܦܩ ܬܘܩܠܬܐ ܡܢ
ܐܘܪܚܐ. ܕܠܐ ܢܟܠܒ ܡܫܘܬܐ ܦܘܠܚܢܬܐ ܘܒܗ ܐܟܣܢܝ̈ܐ
ܕܡܬܬܢܝܢ ܘܢܦܠܝܢ ܐܦ ܗܘ̣ ܢܦܠ ܫܒܝ̈ܬܐ. ܘܟܬܒܘ ܐܦ
ܠܗ ܐ̱ ܥܦܪ ܠܟܘܢ: ܕܢܦܠܐ ܡܢ ܕ̈ܝܪܐ ܕܟܠ ܡܠܦܢܐ
ܠܐ ܡܬܡܠܠܝܢ ܘܫܡܫܐ ܘܠܐ ܡܬܕܒܪܝܢ ܘܡܕܥܐ. ܗܘ̇
ܕܗܘ̣ ܒܕܒܠ ܠܐ ܚܕܕ ܕܢܗܘܐ ܠܗ ܬܠܡܝܕܐ. ܒܢܝ ܟܒܪ
ܬܫ̈ܡܫܬܐ ܦܘܠܚܢܬܐ ܡܢ ܒܬܠ̈ܐ. ܗܠܝܢ ܕܒܗ ܦܫܛ ܠܐ
ܐܟܚܕ ܚܠܡܝܢ. ܦܬܪ ܟܒܪ ܕܠܝܫܐ ܕܠܗ ܡܦܩܢܐ. ܐܝܟ
ܟܒܪ ܒܫܘܪ. ܐܝܟܢܐ ܕܟܬܒܬ ܠܗ ܒܝܡ ܟܝ ܐܝܟ ܬܠܡܝܕܘܗܝ
ܕܥܒܕܗ ܐܒܪܗܡ. ܐܟܪܙܬܐ ܐܝܟܐ ܕܐܦ ܥܫܝܢܐ ܥܕܪܬ ܠܗܘܢ

They related before me that to a certain Jew, who was by the sepulchre of the Patriarchs of the house of Abraham, he said this word, coming up and sitting by him: "Fear not, neither be concerned that thou art called crucifier, for thy lot is with Abraham:" instead of saying "thy portion". Concerning various other blasphemies which he raved and uttered, other men, who disputed with him on this subject and were with him for a long time, but are now in the province of Antioch, have spoken to us, but on account of the extreme shamefulness of these blasphemies it has seemed to me not suitable that they should be stated in this letter.

If therefore he has either written unto you, as I have learned, or has sent unto you his blasphemous books, be careful lest they fall into any person's hands and especially into those of nuns dwelling within church-precincts, lest they be led astray through the simplicity and weakness natural to women. For the wise must all, as is written, "take up the stumbling-block out of the way"[1]), lest he receive many wounds and become the companion of many others who stumble and fall[2]).

Write also to him, if it seem proper to you, that he cease from his blasphemies on an ineffable, pure, incomprehensible and holy doctrine. Concerning which I do not know that he has yet a single disciple, for, of the many arguments which he has collected from the Scriptures, when he applies them, he does not discover the (real) force, but he imagines that they support his view.

I remember that I once wrote to him a letter by means of one of his disciples, Abraham by name; a copy of which also I now send unto you. At that time I did not well know

1) Isaiah LVII, 14.
2) Cf. Isaiah VIII, 15.

ܗܟܢܐ. ܟܕ ܦܠܛ ܠܐ ܡܕܡ ܗܘܬ ܒܗܿܘ ܕܚܠܐ ܕܗܘܐ ܒܠܗ
ܐܡܪܝܢ ܕܝܠܝܦ: ܕܒܦܫܝܛܘܬܐ ܒܠܫܢܐ ܕܠܗ ܕܥܠܝܠ ܡܢ
ܡܢܗܘܪܐ ܦܠܛܬ. ܐܝܟܢܐ ܕܐܦ ܡܫܬܟܡܪ ܘܥܬܕ ܟܠ ܢܦܫܗ
ܒܠܝܢܐ ܘܡܠܘܐ. ܘܕܠܗ ܒܠܫܢܐ ܐܬܡܗܟܬ ܗܕܐ ܕܢܦܬܟܠ
ܫܬܐܫܬ ܠܒܬܟܐ. ܐܝܟܢܐ ܕܐܦ ܠܒܬܟܐ ܦܪܐ ܐܝܠܘܢ
ܫܠܚܐ. ܘܠܦܫܛܘܬܐ ܕܠܗ ܦܪܫܗ ܕܫܠܚܐ. ܗܿܝ ܕܝܢ ܕܝܥܕܪ
ܗܟܢܐ ܬܒ̈ܝܬܐ ܐܦ ܢܬܘܒ ܠܗܘܢ. ܐܝܟ ܕܠܡܠܦܢܘ ܒܦܬܓܡܐ
ܕܬܡܢ ܐܬܦܪܫ. ܥܒܕܬ ܓܝܪ ܕܐܦܢܝ ܠܗܘܢ. ܕܐܦ ܒܐܘܪܗܝ
ܐܬܦܬܠ ܘܠܦܢܝ. ܘܬܘܒ ܐܦ ܡܢ ܦܠܓ ܐܫܬܟܚ. ܒܗܕܐ
ܕܦܠܓܘ ܐܢܫܐ ܡܢ ܕܝܢܐ ܕܬܡܢ ܒܐܦܪܬܐ ܗܕܐ ܕܒܫܪܬ
ܠܗܿ. ܕܗܟܢܐ ܫܕܪܬ ܠܗܘܢ ܢܘܚ̈ܝ: ܘܫܕܒ ܕܦܠܓ ܡܬܒܕܠ
ܡܕܝ. ܡܢ ܗܘܠ ܕܦܠܓܘܢ ܒܐܦܪܬܐ ܗܠܝܢ ܕܠܝ. ܡܕܡ
ܕܡܕܝܢ ܐܝܬܘܢ ܕܦܠܐ ܒܬܘܒ ܠܘܬܗ. ܘܒܟܐ ܒܗ ܘܠܐ
ܥܫܡܥܢܬ ܐܠܐ ܡܥܢܝܬ. ܐܝܟܐ ܓܝܪ ܐܦ ܠܐܦܣܩܦܐ
ܕܐܘܪܫܠܡ ܒܬܪ ܗܘܝܬ ܕܐܬܬܘܒ ܡܬܠܠܗ: ܐܠܐ ܠܐ ܠܐ ܬ̈ܠܠܬܐ
ܕܡܬܠ ܡܫܝܚܘܬܐ: ܘܗܿܝ ܕܠܐ ܡܬܬܘܬܒܝܢ ܠܗ ܫܘܒܚܐ
ܒܡܬܟܬܐ. ܠܘ ܓܝܪ ܥܠܝܠ ܣܓܝܐ ܗܘܐ. ܘܠܘ ܘܒܗܪܬܐ
ܐܢܝ ܗܠܝܢ ܕܢܦܩܠ ܒܗܘܢ. ܠܟ̈ܠܟܐ ܓܝܪ ܘܠܫܪ̈ܝܐ ܘܠܫ̈ܘܬܐ
ܘܠܒܘܪܟܐ ܘܠܒܘܡܒܪܐ ܘܠܥܪ̈ܝܓܐ ܕܐܪܟܐ. ܕܐܬܝܗܘܢ ܒܢܝ
ܚܝܠܐ ܕܐܠܗܐ ܐܡܪ. ܗܘܝܘ ܕܝܢ ܒܬܕܝܢ ܠܡܗܘܐ. ܘܡܬܒܬܥ
ܕܢܦܫ ܠܐܣܝܪ̈ܐ. ܕܗܘܐ ܗܘܐ ܚܝܠܐ ܢܦܩܘܢ. ܘܐܡܪ ܗܘܟܢܐ.
ܕܐܝܟ ܕܐܬܚܘܝܘ، ܐܒܐ ܘܒܪܐ ܘܪܘܚܐ ܚܕ ܚܝܠܐ. ܘܬܘܒ
ܐܦ ܦܠܛܗ ܕܡܠܬܐ ܗܘܝܘ ܒܪ ܚܝܠܐ ܕܐܬܬܘܗܝ. ܦܠܛܝܦ
ܕܝܢ ܐܦ ܠܘܬ ܗܕܐ ܡܠܝܠܘܬܐ ܡܢ ܠܐ ܡܕܒܪܢܘܬܗ ܗܝܡܢܐ

that he had dared to imagine such blasphemies, for I had only met with his commentaries on a few of the Psalms, in which he also glorifies himself and ascribes to himself revelations and visions, and (says) that to him alone is it given to understand the Scriptures correctly. In them he also calls the Scriptures dreams, and his commentaries the interpretation of dreams.

Afterwards he craftily devised to send his books to you and to write to you, in order to deceive the simple people there (at Jerusalem); for I have heard that he says to them, that even in Edessa is his heresy received, and is furthermore much praised by us, — until some of the monks there happened upon the letter which I had written, of which I now send you a copy, and found that (on the contrary) he was strongly censured by me. When therefore you shall have received these letters of mine, that which you know to be just write unto him, and reprove him, and that not feebly but forcibly. I myself would write to the bishop of Jerusalem [1]) respecting him, were it not for differences concerning the faith, and that the fact of our not being of the same communion is a middle wall (of partition) between us [2]). For this man has sinned not a little, and the offences which he has committed are not small; for he says that dogs, pigs, serpents, scorpions, mice, and other reptiles of the earth, are consubstantial with God: that is will become so. He also strives to persuade others to believe likewise, and says thus: "As the Father and the Son and the Spirit are of one nature, and as the body of the Word is consubstantial with his divinity", through ignorance he also blasphemes concerning this part (of Church doctrine), adding, "all creation also will

1) Elias, Patriarch of Jerusalem.

2) Ephesians II, 14.

ܘܐܡܪ. ܕܐܦ ܟܠ ܒܪܝܬܐ ܥܬܝܕܐ ܕܬܗܘܐ ܒܪܬ ܟܝܢܐ ܟܝܢܐ
ܕܐܠܗܘܬܐ. ܘܚܪܫܐ ܘܩܛܘܠܐ. ܘܙܩܘܦܐ ܘܫܠܝܚܐ.
ܘܪܕܘܦܐ ܘܣܗܕܐ. ܘܓܝܪܐ ܘܒܬܘܠܬܐ. ܘܡܣܝܒܪܢܐ
ܘܡܠܝ ܐܪܓܬܐ. ܟܠܗܘܢ ܐܡܪ ܕܐܫܬܢܝ
ܡܬܬܠܝܢ ܘܗܘܝܢ ܚܕ ܟܝܢܐ ܥܡ ܐܠܗܐ.
ܘܠܐ ܗܘ ܕܐܝܬ ܠܗ ܡܬܝܬܪ.
ܘܠܐ ܐܢܫܐ ܕܚܣܝܪ ܠܗ
ܡܬܚܣܪ. ܟܕ. ܘܟ

become consubstantial with the Divine nature": and magicians and murderers, crucifiers and apostles, persecutors and martyrs, adulterers and virgins, the chaste and those who satisfy their lusts, all, he says, will be changed and become consubstantial with God, and there will be no one who shall excel, neither any one who shall be lacking [1]).

---

1) It seems either that at this point a sheet of the MS. was lost before it was bound, or that the MS. from which this copy was made was a defective one.

V.

THE PHILOSOPHIC SYSTEM OF BAR SUDAILI.

The letter of Jacob of Sarug was evidently written at a period when Bar Sudaili had not yet thrown off the mask entirely: it makes no mention of pantheistic doctrines, but simply upholds the church doctrine of the eternity of punishment against Bar Sudaili's theory of its temporal duration. In doing so he falls, Jacob of Takrit (XIII century) remarks [1]), into the error of the Semi-Pelagians, that the just received eternal bliss because God foreknew that they would always have continued in righteousness. This view cannot be correctly said to be that of the Semi-Pelagians, although it resembles it in the coöperation of the two elements of grace and good works.

Philoxenos has confined himself, in his letter, to treating in general terms of one part only of Bar Sudaili's system, that which seemed to him most pernicious, his pantheism and his doctrine of salvation. His system was openly pantheistic, or, to speak more philosophically, *Pan-nihilistic;* for, according to him, all nature even to the lowest forms of animal

1) The passage is in his ܟܬܒܐ ܕܣܝܡܬܐ »Book of Treasures" (written in 1231), part III, ch. 39: cf. Assem. B. O., T. II, p. 240; and Abbeloos, S. Jacques de Sarug, p. 125.

creation, being simply an emanation from the Divinity-Chaos [1]), finally returns to it; and, when the consummation has taken place, God himself passes away and everything is swallowed up in the indefinite chaos which he conceives to be the first principle and the end of being, and which admits of no distinction. Let us examine the salient features to be noticed in Philoxenos' letter, and compare them with the doctrines of the Book of Hierotheos as they are disclosed in the summary given further on. In the first place, we read that Bar Sudaili "openly assimilates the creation to God and teaches that it is necessary for everything to become like him" [2]): his formula was, »All nature is consubstantial with the Divinity" [3]). Secondly, there are three periods of existence: 1. the present world, which is evil, and to which belongs motion: 2. during this period all existence is brought into complete union with Christ who »is all and in all men"; this is the period of rest and liberty: 3. finally, all nature becomes of the same nature with the universal essence [4]). This is the consummation or the confusion of all things, when distinction disappears, not only between God and Nature, but between the persons of the Godhead itself [5]): God, as personality, passes away, and there is no longer Father, Son, and Spirit. Even the devils are finally redeemed, and included in the general indistinction and confusion [6]). This doctrine of universal redemption and return into the divine nature — the *ἀποκατάστασις* — was, as is well known, the common doctrine of the great Alexandrian and Antiochene schools. Both Origen and Theodore of Mopsuestia, like

---

1) His first principle is identical with the Θεαρχία or source of divinity of Pseudo-Dionysios.

2) P. 28. 3) P. 42. 4) P. 32 seq.

5) P. 34. 6) P. 32.

Bar Sudaili, assign three periods to rational existence: the present; that when all existence is united in Christ; and the final absorption or ἀποκατάστασις; the only difference being that with Theodore this was final, whereas with Origen this process was continually repeated. The same doctrine was taught by Gregory of Nyssa on the one hand and Diodoros of Tarsos on the other.

The Book of Hierotheos takes precisely the same standpoint. In it, the emanation from the Good comprehends all the grades of nature down to the lowest, including also the fallen evil spirits [1]. The redemption of the hell-sphere and of Satan is taught in detail: we even see, from the commentary of Theodosios, that this point in the Book of Hierotheos had excited much comment and reprobation among theologians [2], and that it was considered by them, as by Philox-

---

1) See p. 110. 2) Comm. on Book IV, ch. 17, which is entitled ܥܠ ܬܝܒܘܬܐ ܕܬܚܬܝ̈ܐ. ܦܢܩܝܬܐ »On the repentance of those below".
ܣܓܝ̈ܐܐ ܓܝܪ ܡܢ ܒܝ̈ܫܐ ܕܗܘܘ ܡܡܠܠܢܐ ܕܐܪܬܕܘܟܣܘܬܐ ܒܥܕܬܐ
ܕܐܠܗܐ. ܚܫܒܘ ܥܠ ܗܢܐ ܡܠܦܢܐ ܐܝܪܘܬܐܘܣ ܕܟܕ ܐܟܬܒ
ܠܡܠܐܘܗܝ ܗܢܐ ܥܠ ܬܝܒܘܬܐ ܕܬܚܬܝ̈ܐ. ܕܡܛܠ ܬܝܒܘܬܐ
ܕܫܐ̈ܕܐ ܐܡܪ: ܠܐ ܗܘܐ ܓܝܪ ܡܛܠ ܬܝܒܘܬܐ ܕܫܐ̈ܕܐ
ܗܠܝܢ ܐܡܪ. ܐܦܠܐ ܢܚܫܐ ܕܐܝܟ ܗܢܐ ܢܣܒ ܗܘܐ
ܡܠܦܢܐ. ܐܠܐ ܡܛܠ ܒܝ̈ܫܐ ܕܚܙܝܐ ܒܥܬܝܕܘܬܗ ܠܐܬܘܪܬܐ
ܕܫܐ̈ܕܐ. ܘܗܕܐ ܚܕܐ ܦܠܓܐ ܕܡܛܠ ܬܝܒܘܬܐ ܕܒܝ̈ܫܐ
ܐܡܪ. ܡܢ ܗܿܝ ܕܐܡܪ« ܕܒܡܬܬܐ ܕܐܦ̈ܩܝ ܒܫܘܬܗ ܡܢ ܫܘܠ
ܕܒܝܢܬܐ ܘܫܘܪܐ ܘܡܢ ܐܪܥܘܬܐ ܕܡܫܚܠܦܐ ܠܗ«. ܐܪܥܘܬܐ ܕܝܢ
ܠܥܕܬܐ ܦܪܐ ܕܠܒܝ̈ܫܐ ܡܫܚܠܦ: »Now many among the mystical divines of the church of God have considered that Hierotheos when he wrote this chapter »on the repentance of those below" meant the repent-

enos, a dangerous point, for Theodosios vainly endeavors to clear Hierotheos from the charge. This fact itself is of importance from its connection with the criticisms of Philoxenos on Bar Sudaili.

The three periods which Philoxenos finds in Bar Sudaili clearly appear in Hierotheos, not only as world-periods but as phases of the development of individual souls. The first or natural condition is that during which the mind aspires with motion towards the first principle, but still possesses evil in itself. The second takes place when the mind or rational nature, through its rise, becomes identified with Christ and goes through its long experience and purification before reaching the final consummation, experience during which it performs all the acts of Christ and is Christ himself; for Christ is nothing but the Universal Mind. The third state is when all nature is completely absorbed into the original chaos from which all originally sprang, even God himself: in this absorption, Father, Son, and Spirit disappear, and all distinction vanishes [1]).

Any further details at this point seem unnecessary; a reading of the summary of the Book will show even more clearly the complete identity of Bar Sudaili's doctrine, so far as it is stated by Philoxenos, with that of the Book of Hierotheos. If the analogy went only so far as to cover what is, so to speak, the common ground of pantheistic mysticism, there would be nothing remarkable or conclusive in such a coincidence. What would seem, however, to be a strong argument for the identity of the two writers, —

---

ance of demons. But our teacher did not say these things of the repentance of demons, nor had he any such thing in mind: on the contrary it was of those men whose evil had led them into the abode of demons. This fact is clear and evident, that he spoke of the repentance of men, from his saying," etc.

1) See summary of Book of Hierotheos.

besides the three world-periods, — is the form of doctrine found in both on the „consummation": what other mystic writer had ever dared to reach such a depth of logical blasphemy as to assert in so many words that „the Father, Son, and Spirit", that God, will cease to exist? This is, of course, but the logical consequence of the Pseudo-Dionysian doctrine of an emanated Trinity, for, as Origen says, „as the beginning is, so must the end be"; but nowhere in these writings, any more than in those of the Alexandrian and Antiochene doctors who teach the *ἀποκατάστασις*, is such a consequence expressed. Many striking personal similarities between Bar Sudaili and Pseudo-Hierotheos are evident at first sight: both lay claim to direct divine revelations; both make extensive use of Scripture for the support of their theories. It remains for us to see whether the Dionysian fragments of Hierotheos are in accord with what has been deduced. As it would be out of place to give here their full text, which would have to be compared with passages of the Book of Hierotheos, a few words of description will be sufficient. The extract from the *Elements of Theology* [1]) is a definition of the nature of Christ. The divinity of Jesus (*τοῦ Ἰησοῦ θεότης*) is the all-including cause, above intelligence, life, and substance. It maintains the harmony of the parts and the whole, being above both the parts and the whole. Between this conception and that of Christ as the *universal essence* and the *union* of all things, the harmony is evident. The extract given in *Eccles. Hier.* (ch. II, 1) shows that „*the first motion of the mind towards the divine is the love of God*"; and the fragments from the *Erotic hymns* [2]) treat of love as a unitive force moving all beings „*from the Good*

1) Divine Names, ch. II, 10. 2) Divine Names, ch. IV, 15—17.

down to the last of beings and from the last of beings up to the Good". There are many corresponding passages in Hierotheos: he describes the motion of glorifying and loving, as that which belongs to distinct and separate existence, as the supplication of those who have fallen. "All rational essences glorify and love the essence from which they were separated".

It seems at first difficult to explain why Philoxenos pours such fierce invectives on Bar Sudaili, and stigmatizes his doctrines as unheard of, and worse than Judaism or Heathenism. Although they were expressed in bold language by Bar Sudaili, yet, besides being in accord with the prevailing spirit of East-Syrian and Egyptian monasticism, how many famous teachers and doctors of the church had supported the same doctrine! While it is presented in different forms by Sabellios [1]), Marcellus of Ankyra [2]), etc., it is upheld by the whole Alexandrian School, by Clement, Origen, and Didymos, by Gregory Nazianzen [3]) and Gregory of Nyssa, by Nemesios, Synesios, and others, and later by the School of Antioch, headed by Diodoros of Tarsos and Theodore of Mopsuestia. Among the East-Syrians even S. Ephraem can hardly be cleared from the stain of a moderate mystical pantheism. If none of these theologians used the same freedom of language as Bar Sudaili, on approaching the most sacred precincts of the Christian faith, Philoxenos must have been too subtle a theologian not to have seen beyond their reticences. The severity shown to Stephen cannot then be explained from the principles of his thought, but from the freedom of his language, which was such as to throw oblo-

---

1) See Neander, I, pp. 598 and 600.
2) Adversus Marc.: see Dorner, I. 2, p. 282.
3) E. g. his hymn published in notes to Dionysios (Op. om. ed. Migne, I. p. 606).

quy on the whole mystical school and to draw upon it the reprobation of ecclesiastical authority. Another explanation, the plausibility of which may appear further on, would be Bar Sudaili's connection with the beginning of the well-known Origenistic revival in the first part of the VI century.

VI.

BIOGRAPHY OF BAR SUDAILI.

The biographical information concerning Bar Sudaili at our disposal is very meagre. Philoxenos tells us that he was a native of Edessa and a ܣܦܪܐ or scribe, and Jacob of Sarug shows him to have been a monk of considerable repute for sanctity and good works; in fact, the terms of praise which he bestows on Bar Sudaili indicate that, until then, the latter enjoyed the favor of the Monophysite party, though already he had not only begun to show his anti-christian sentiments more openly, but was also cherishing ambitious aims. In all probability Bar Sudaili passed a portion of his early career in Egypt, for Philoxenos mentions his having followed for some time the leadership of John the Egyptian. If his identity with Pseudo-Hierotheos be granted, there would be some interesting traces of this early part of his life. Three dogmatic extracts passing under the name of Hierotheos are preserved, in either Arabic or Ethiopic versions; the originals seem to have been in Coptic. Two of these appear in the well-known *Fides Patrum* [1]), a work compiled probably in

1) The Arabic version is found in the Vatican (Arabic Cod. 101 ff. 11 and 12), in Florence (Medic. Palat. Library C.LXIX) and in the Vict. Emanuel Lib. at Rome. The Ethiopic text is preserved in the Brit. Mus. Ethiopic Cod. 14 Add. 16,219 f. 7—8, and in the Library of the Univ. of Tübingen.

the XI cent.: a Latin version of them was given by Mai in tome III of his *Spicilegium Romanum* (p. 704) [1]), but both the Arabic and Ethiopic texts have remained inedited. These fragments, which contain declarations concerning the nature of Christ, are somewhat colorless, although perceptibly Monophysite [2]). Of more interest is a confession of faith, contained in an Arabic MS. of the councils (Arab. Vatic. 409 f. 397), which seems not to have been noticed by Mai. Here a strong pantheistic and mystical tinge is added to its Monophysitism, and many expressions remind us of Bar Sudaili, especially those in which the all-containing nature of the *thearchy* is taught [3]).

It appears clearly from the language of these fragments that they were written at a time when the Monophysite controversy was at its height; and the probabilities are in favor of their having been written by Bar Sudaili. The first two show him to have been at first a prudent but evident Monophysite, and the last must have been produced somewhat later, when his creed had become more mystical. There are no traces of them in Syriac, and they must without any doubt be referred to a residence in Egypt. It was in Edessa however that he began to show his personal views: it is probable that he was still in that city when Jacob of Sarug adressed to him the present letter. Then also Philoxenos may have written to him the previous letter which he refers to, and the copy of which he enclosed [4]). Soon after, in all probability from the opposition he met with in his native city,

1) Mai published it without pledging himself in any way, »nullum interponens de iis judicium".

2) Compare their phraseology with that of Jacob of Sarug, e. g. in his letter to the monks of Bassus.

3) I intend to publish the text of these documents with that of the Book of Hierotheos. 4) See pp. 44—47.

Bar Sudaili was obliged to leave Edessa and betake himself to Palestine, where the greater freedom of thought allowed was abundantly used by the Origenistic monks, who were growing numerous and bold. At or near Jerusalem he entered a monastery, as we see from the letter of Philoxenos: that he was ever an abbot seems to be a gratuitous assumption on the part of Neander, Gfrörer, and those who have copied the assertion from them. We have no record of his being expelled from this monastery, as some were, in consequence of his scandalously pantheistic views, but there can be no doubt that they became well-known, not only from his writings, but also from the words he wrote on the wall of his cell, „All nature is consubstantial with the Divinity". About the same time we hear of the expulsion, for Origenistic views, of four monks from the new Laura of S. Saba, with the consent of the archbishop Elias [1]), to whom also Philoxenos, in his letter, speaks of appealing: it would not therefore have been surprising if Bar Sudaili had been treated in the same manner. The period of his residence in Jerusalem is the only part of his career which may be dated with approximate certainty, between the years 494 and 512, from the concordance of dates between Jacob of Sarug (b. 454, d. 522), Philoxenos (485—518), and Elias of Jerusalem (494—513). As Philoxenos refers to the impossibility of his communicating with the Patriarch of Jerusalem on account of their division in faith, we are inclined to narrow the period at which his letter was written to between 509 and 512, when the contest between the two parties was at its height. Another chronological indication might be found in the ܗܝܦܣܘܬܐ,

1) Cyrillus Scythopolita, Vita S. Sabae.

„Confession of faith", of Philoxenos [1]), if the period at which it was written could be exactly determined; for in the anathema at the close he enumerates ܒܪ ܨܘܕܝܠܐ ܪܫܝܥܐ „the impious Bar Sudaili". This confession may have been drawn up at the synod of Sidon, held in 512—513, of which Philoxenos was the prime mover. In the profession of faith [2]) demanded, among the Jacobites, of priests and deacons on their receiving orders, we also read the anathematism of Bar Sudaili and his followers. Stephen had evidently become a man of importance and influence.

Bar ʿEbraia, in his Ecclesiastical History [3]), makes Bar Sudaili flourish at Edessa under the Antiochene patriarch Sergios, the successor of Severos, about 542. This is at variance with all our other evidence, and is certainly an error; for Stephen had already left Edessa, as we have seen, during the first years of the century, and his career could hardly have lasted until the middle of it.

It would be of great interest to know from what source

---

1) Brit. Mus. Add. 17216: cf. Wright's Cat., II, 533. Cod. Syr. Vat. CLIX, f. 83, v. ܟܕ ܡܚܪܡܝܢ ܠܟܠܗܘܢ ܡ̈ܡܠܠܝ ܡܣܩܒܠܘܬܐ ܕܟܝܢ ܐܦ ܡܫܠܡܢܘܬܐ ܘܪܫܝܥܘܬܐ ܦܠܠܐ ܠܗܘܦܟܐ ܗܘ̄ ܫܠܝܚܘܬܐ ܕܐܬܪ̈ܝܢ ܥܘܒܕܐ. ܕܐܬܬܗܘܢ ..... ܘܡܬܗܘܐ: ܘܡܕܪܐ: ܘܡܫܝܚܝܢ ܕܐܟܠܘܗ ܘܒܪ ܨܘܕܝܠܐ ܪܫܝܥܐ: ܘܐܡܘܣ ܦܘܪܗܣܐ: ܘܫ̄ܪ.

2) Cod. Syr. Vat. XLIX, f. 58. It anathematizes ܘܠܐܘܪܝܓܢܐ ܒܪ ܨܘܕܐܝܠܐ. ܘܠܟܠܗܘܢ ܕܐܡܪܝܢ ܕܫܠܡܐ ܗܘܐ ܠܗ ܠܕܝܢ ܘܐܟܠܗܘܢ ܡܟܢܐ ܐܫܝܢܐ. ܐܘ ܡܕܡ ܐܚܪܢܐ ܡܢ ܗܠܝܢ ܕܦܐܝܢ ܠܐܠܗܘܬܐ ܟܝܢܐ ܡܢ ܐܠܦܝܢ ✣

3) Ed. Abbeloos and Lamy, p. 215. Cf. Assem. B. O., T. II, p. 327.

Bar Sudaili derived a part at least of his doctrines. On this point we find an interesting fact noted by Philoxenos in these words: „*He desired .... to originate heresies himself also, like John the Egyptian, whom for a short time he even followed*" [1]). His master then, before he came forward as an original thinker, was a John of Egypt. At this period the monophysite monk John II (509—517) was Patriarch of Alexandria; but as his relations with Severos of Antioch and the Syrian Monophysites were intimate, it is hardly possible that Philoxenos should have referred to him. Bar ᶜEbraia includes a John of Egypt in his enumeration of the Monophysites who flourished under Sergios of Antioch [2]); but I have not met with any other notice which could with safety be referred to him. The John of Alexandria spoken of in Zacharias Rhetor as a heretic and falsifier of writings is, in all probability, another and an earlier writer [3]). In no case could we identify this John with the Syrian John of Egypt, bishop of ܐܣܝܐ, whose life is given by John of Asia [4]); for, besides the fact that he flourished at a slightly later period, had he held the opinions which a master of Bar Sudaili must have had and which Philoxenos indicates, John of Asia, belonging to the same party as Philoxenos, would never have enumerated him among his saintly personages. It is hardly necessary, however, to question the opinions of this master of Bar Sudaili: the mystical pantheism of the monks of Egypt and Syria from the IV to the VI century, as well as the intimate relations between the two countries, are facts too well-known to require proof. In both there flourished every degree of pantheism and pan-nihilism, from the gross and

1) See pp. 32—3. 2) Assemani B. O., T. II, p. 327.
3) Land, Anecdota Syriaca, T. II, p. 177.
4) Land, op. cit. T. III, p. 130.

material form of the Euchites to the spiritualized forms of the kabbalistic, Neo-platonic and Origenistic sects. Late researches tend to show that much of this was engrafted from the old Egyptian sects, with slight transformations required by the new dispensation. How much of this earlier form was embodied in the so-called Hermetic books it is difficult to determine, as they seem to be the work of such different periods.

Stephen bar Sudaili was undoubtedly in many points a follower of Origen and the Alexandrian school, but his thought was dominated by gnostico-kabbalistic elements. Having boldly proclaimed his doctrines, he sought to propagate them by numerous writings. Philoxenos shows him to have been a learned man, much devoted to the study of Scripture, which he interpreted in a kabbalistic manner, carrying probably to excess the mania for this kind of exegesis, which was in vogue among the followers and imitators of Origen; although it did not originate with the latter, but is found even more elaborated in the writings of Philo.

Although Philoxenos speaks of letters, commentaries, books, and other writings of Bar Sudaili, he gives details only regarding an early one, the first which came into his hands, a commentary on the Psalms. In it Stephen claimed to have direct revelations and to be an inspired man, to whom *alone* was revealed the true sense of Scripture: he called them dreams and his commentaries on them the interpretations of dreams. Philoxenos indicates that in this work Bar Sudaili had not yet developed his pantheism. The question naturally arises, was he acquainted with the Book of Hierotheos and did he make use of it in his criticisms? It seems as if this were not the case: otherwise the language of Philoxenos would have been entirely different. As it is, the phraseology shows that he had other sources of information. He refers in particular to a book in which Stephen sets forth his doctrines (pp. 42—43) in a language which, he says, is entirely inadequate to the subject, *"insipid and foolish"*. From this book he extracts most of the statements which he condemns. What other works of Bar Sudaili he may have seen, it does not appear. Had he known of the imposture perpetrated by Stephen, he would not have failed to publicly accuse him of it: the secret character of the Book of Hierotheos must for some time have prevented its existence being generally known, even if it had been already written at that time.

From several passages in Philoxenos it appears that Bar Sudaili must have made numerous and active disciples (though he seeks to deny it), and have kept up continuous relations with Edessa, where he boasted of having adherents. We find that Philoxenos himself, before becoming acquainted with Stephen's most reprehensible doctrines, wrote to him a letter — now lost — which he sent by one of Stephen's disciples named Abraham: and the reason which induced Philoxenos to write to Abraham and Orestes at Edessa was, that they had received from Bar Sudaili letters and other works, sent to them through some of his followers; by which he wished to seduce them, and probably others, to adopt his pernicious doctrines.

Thus much have we been able to collect respecting Bar Sudaili: now it will be necessary, in order to complete his biography, to pass to the question of his identity with Pseudo-Hierotheos.

VII.

BAR SUDAILI CONSIDERED BY SYRIAN WRITERS TO BE THE AUTHOR OF THE BOOK OF HIEROTHEOS.

It has already been stated by Asseman [1]) that Gregory Bar ʿEbraia the monophysite patriarch (XIII cent.) asserted the great work of Bar Sudaili to have been that entitled the Book of Hierotheos. The passage referred to is in his work entitled, ܡܢܪܬ ܩܘܕܫܐ [2]). In giving an enumeration of heresies on the Incarnation, he assigns the last place to Bar Sudaili, saying [3]): *"Thirtieth heresy; that of Stephen*

1) B. O., T. II, p. 290—291.

2) ܡܢܪܬ ܩܘܕܫܐ ܡܛܠ ܫܬܐܣ̈ܬܐ ܥܕܬܢܝ̈ܬܐ, at the end of the IV *foundation*; cf. Asseman, ibid.

3) ܗܪܣܝܣ ܕܬܠܬܝܢ ܗܝ ܕܐܣܛܦܐܢܐ ܒܪ ܨܘܕ ܐܝ̈ܠܐ. ܗܢܐ ܐܡܪ ܕܐܝܬ ܫܘܠܡܐ ܠܬܫܢܝܩܐ. ܘܕܠܘ ܠܥܠܡ ܒܠܚܘܕ ܡܫܬܘܚܪܝܢ ܕ̈ܝܢܐ. ܐܠܐ ܒܢܘܪܐ ܡܬܕܟܝܢ. ܘܗܟܢܐ ܐܦ ܫ̈ܐܕܐ ܡܬܚܣܝܢ. ܘܠܡܬܕܡ ܠܚܢܐ ܐܠܗܝܐ ܡܛܠ ܐܝܟ ܕܐܡܪ ܦܘܠܘܣ ܕܢܗܘܐ ܐܠܗܐ ܟܠ ܒܟܠ. ܘܬܒܥܐ ܐܬܒܥܬ ܡܛܠ ܫܘܪܪܐ ܕܗܢܐ ܬܪܥܝܬܐ. ܘܡܫܟܚܗ ܕܐܝܬܘܗܝ ܪܒܗ ܕܡܕܝܢܐ ܕܐܘܣܘܣܘܣ ܩܝܘܡܝ. ܒܐܓܪܬ ܐܝܟ ܗܘ ܕܕܠܗ ܗܘ ܒܐܓܪܬ ܕܡܕܝܢܐ ܐܝܬܘܗܝ. ܐܦ ܦܫܝ̈ܩܬܐ ܗܘܝܐ ܡܥܒܪܢ.

bar Sudaili He affirmed that there will be an end to the torments (of hell), and that the wicked will not suffer forever, but will be purified by fire. Thus will mercy be shewn even to demons, and everything will return into the Divine nature, as Paul says, "God will be all in all". He also wrote a book in support of this opinion, and called it by the name of Hierotheos, the master of the holy Dionysios, as if it were by the holy Hierotheos himself; which many also think".

In a second passage, in the first section of his *Ecclesiastical History* [1]), Bar ʿEbraia speaks of Stephen, but adds nothing new, except that he mentions his Scripture-commentaries. His words are: [2]) *"At this time Stephen bar Sudaili became notorious as a monk in Edessa. He interpreted the Scriptures according to his own ideas, and affirmed that there will be an end to the torments of hell, and that sinners and even demons will be justified; laying down as the foundation of his teaching that, as Paul says, "God will be all in all"*.

These few words represent in an absolutely exact manner the teachings of Bar Sudaili as related by Philoxenos, but the most important point is the categorical assertion, that Bar Sudaili attempted to palm off his principal work as that of Hierotheos, the supposed master of Dionysios the Areopagite. Were this statement only the expression of Bar ʿEbraia's

---

1) Ed. Abbeloos and Lamy, p. 222. 2) ܘܒܗ ܒܙܒܢܐ ܐܦ ܐܣܛܦܢܐ ܒܪ ܨܘܕܝܠܝ ܢܕܥ ܒܐܘܪܗܝ، ܕܝܪܝܐ ܒܘܢܝܐ. ܘܦܫܩ ܠܟܬ̈ܒܐ ܡܢ ܢܦܫܗ. ܘܫܘܠܡܐ ܐܡܪ ܠܫܘܢܩܐ. ܘܕܡܙܕܕܩܝܢ ܚ̈ܛܝܐ ܘܕܡܐ ܕܐܦ ܫ̈ܐܕܐ. ܟܕ ܣܡ ܗ̇، ܕܢܗܘܐ ܐܠܗܐ ܟܠ ܒܟܠ ܐܝܟ ܕܐܡܪ ܦܘܠܘܣ. ܗܢܐ ܫܬܐܣܬܐ ܕܡܠܦܢܘܬܗ.

personal opinion, one could but feel considerable hesitation in accepting the conclusions of a writer who lived more than seven centuries after the one whom he criticises; and until now the assertion has been supposed to rest entirely with him [1]. The case assumes a different aspect when, in another of his writings, Bar 'Ebraia quotes in support of his view a writer of the VIII century, Kyriakos Patriarch of Antioch (793—817). This passage occurs in the ***Nomocanon*** or ܟܬܒܐ ܕܗܘܕܝܐ ܡܛܠ ܩܢܘܢܐ ܥܕܬܢܝܐ ܘܢܡܘܣܐ ܥܠܡܢܝܐ "*The Book of Directions concerning ecclesiastical Canons and civil laws*". In ch. VII, sect. 9 [2], in which he enumerates the canonical and apocryphal Scriptures, etc., after speaking of apocryphal revelations of the apostles John, Paul, Peter, etc., he gives a sentence of Kyriakos on the book of Hierotheos in these terms: ܩܘܪܝܩܘܣ ܦܛܪܝܪܟܐ. ܟܬܒܐ ܗܘ ܕܪܫܝܡ ܕܐܝܪܘܬܐܘܣ. ܠܐ ܕܝܠܗ ܗܘ ܐܠܐ ܕܡܣܒܪܐ ܕܐܣܛܦܢܘܣ ܒܪ ܨܘܕ ܐ̈ܝܠܐ ܗܪܛܝܩܐ ܐܝܬܘܗܝ. "*The patriarch Kyriakos (says): The book entitled (that) of **Hierotheos** is not by him but probably by the heretic Stephen Bar Sudaili*".

Bar 'Ebraia might have quoted another writer, who also lived in the VIII and IX centuries, John bishop of Dara, whose testimony is of the greater value in that he was a noted mystic and a student of the writings of preceding mystics, especially those of Pseudo-Dionysios. Beside his book on the Celestial and Ecclesiastical Hierarchies, already mentioned, he wrote an important work on the soul [3] and another on the resurrection of the body [4]. The latter,

1) This is the opinion of Neander, Dorner, and all who have treated the subject.

2) Cod. Syr. Vat. CXXXII, f. 32: cf. Assemani B. O., T. II, p. 302, and Catal. T. III, p. 199.

3) Assem. B. O., T. II, pp. 219, 505.

4) Cod. Syr. Vat. C. Cf. Assem. Cat. T. II, p. 530.

entitled ܥܠ ܩܝܡܬܐ ܕܦܓܪ̈ܐ ܐܢܫ̈ܝܐ ܒܡܐܡܪ̈ܐ ܐܪܒܥܐ, „*Four books on the resurrection of human bodies*", is a work of great interest and learning: in it he devotes a chapter (l. IV, c. 21) to supporting the eternity of Paradise and Hell [1]). The opening sentence is worth quoting: „*Diodoros of Tarsos in the book which he wrote on the Œconomy, and Theodore his disciple and the master of Nestorios, say in many places that there is an end to condemnation. The same course is also taken by the work called the Book of Hierotheos, which is in reality not by him but was skilfully written by another in his name, that is by Stephen bar Sudaili. Gregory of Nyssa also, in his book* ܡܪܬܝܢܐ *and in that to his sister Makrina, and in other compositions, teaches the dogma of apokatastasis, that is, the return into the first principle, and says that there will be an end to future torments. However, all the doctors of the church, Greeks as well as Syrians, with the sole exception of this saint, say unanimously that there will be no end to the torments of hell* [2])."

---

1) Cod. C. f. 69, v. Cf. ibid. p. 537—8.

2) ܕܕܝܘܕܘܪܘܣ ܡ̣ܢ ܗ̣ܘ ܕܛܪܣܘܣ ܒܟܬܒܐ ܗܘ ܕܡܦܪܢܣܢܘܬܐ ܕܐܟܬܒ̀ ܘܬܐܕܘܪܘܣ ܬܠܡܝܕܗ ܕܗܘܝܐ ܘܪܒܗ ܕܢܣܛܘܪܝܘܣ: ܒܕܘܟܝ̈ܬܐ ܣܓܝ̈ܐܬܐ ܐܡܪ̈ܝܢ ܕܐܝܬ ܫܘܠܡܐ ܠܕܝܢܐ. ܗ̇ܢ ܟܐܘܪܚܐ ܐܦ ܘܟܬܒܐ ܗ̇ܘ ܕܡܬܩܪܐ ܕܐܝܪܬܐܘܣ. ܕܕܠܗ ܠܐ ܐܝܬܘܗ̇ܝ، ܫܪܝܪܬ. ܡ̣ܢ ܐܚܪܢܐ ܕ̣ܗܘ ܐܬܚܟܡ ܥܠ ܫܡܗ. ܘܗ̇ܘ ܕܐܣܛܦܢܐ ܒܪ ܨܘܕܝܠܐ. ܗܟܘܬ ܬܘܒ ܘܓܪܝܓܘܪܝܘܣ ܕܢܘܣܐ ܒܡܐܡܪܐ ܗܘ ܡܪܬܝܢܐ ܕܥܠܗ ܘܒܗܘ ܕܠܘܬ ܡܩܪܝܢܐ ܚܬܗ. ܘܒܡܟܬܒܢܘ̈ܬܐ ܐܚܪ̈ܢܝܬܐ ܡܠܦ ܠܕܘܓܡܐ ܗ̇ܘ ܕܐܦܘܟܛܐܣܛܐܣܝܣ ܐܘܟܝܬ ܦܢܝܐ

In the same chapter John of Dara quotes, among other authorities in favor of the eternity of punishment, the letter of Jacob of Sarug to Stephen. His long extract extends from p. 18, l. 16 of the text, to p. 24, l. 10, and covers nearly the same ground as the extract, in Add. 17,193, of which we have given the various readings under the letter D.

These two authorities flourished between two and three centuries after Bar Sudaili, and it is easy to perceive that there must have been a continuous tradition among Syrian church writers on the subject; a tradition which is of the greatest authority even taken by itself, and if in accord with the intrinsic evidence would seem to be incontestable. It is clear, from what precedes, that this work took a very prominent position, and exercised a strong influence over the different schools of thought.

Having reached this point in my researches on Bar Sudaili, I made every attempt to discover traces of the Book of Hierotheos. Father P. Halloix wrote a life of Hierotheos for his collection of lives of Eastern church writers of the first two centuries [1], but in it were used only the fragments quoted

---

ܕܡܫܬܪܝܢ: ܘܐܡܪ ܕܐܝܬ ܫܘܠܡܐ ܠܬܫܢܝܩܐ ܗܘ ܕܒܬܪܟܢ.
ܫ̈ܠܡܘܬܐ ܕܝܢ ܕܒܬܪܟܢ ܘܡ̈ܘܬܒܐ ܒܝܬ ܘܣܘܪ̈ܚܢܐ ܗܦܟ ܡܢ ܗܢܐ
ܡܬܚܙܝܐ ܠܡܫܘܕܘܗܝ، ܥܠܝܗܘܢ ܫܘܝܐܝܬ ܐܡܪܝܢ ܕܠܝܬ ܫܘܠܡܐ
ܠܬܫܢܝܩܐ ܗܘ.

1) Illustrium Ecclesiae Orientalis Scriptorum vitæ et documenta. Duaci 1633, p. 600—634. The so-called life is made up of quotations from mediæval writers. The commemoration in the Menaei of the Greek church shows what superstitious reverence was accorded to the shadowy personality of Hierotheos, known to them only through the medium of Dionysios.

by Pseudo-Dionysios: the other references were valueless as independent testimony, for they were all derived from the Pseudo-Dionysian writings. Halloix had no knowledge whatever of any Book of Hierotheos, or of a possible connection between Pseudo-Hierotheos and Bar Sudaili, but believed implicitly in the existence of a first century writer. Researches among Greek and Latin MSS. were also of no avail. I found, however, that there still existed at the British Museum a unique MS. of the book of Hierotheos in Syriac. It was described, but erroneously, in Rosen and Forshall's catalogue as translated and commentated by Theodosios Patriarch of Antioch, the second alone being the case. This work I was enabled to copy.

VIII.

THE BOOK OF HIEROTHEOS.

As already remarked, this Book pretends to have been written by a certain holy man of the first century, Hierotheos, a disciple of S. Paul and teacher of Dionysios the Areopagite, to whom also the work is supposed to be addressed. Legend tells us that he was the first bishop of Athens, before Dionysios, and that he afterwards went to Spain, where he remained as bishop. Dionysios says that he was present with the apostles at the death of the Virgin, and became noted for his beautiful hymns.

To return to our subject: this work is extant only in Syriac, in connection with an extensive commentary by Theodosios, patriarch of Antioch at the close of the IX century (887—896), in a unique MS. of the British Museum belonging, in great part, to the XIII century [1]. This is the very copy which, after great labor, Bar ʿEbraia succeeded in procuring, and from which he composed a compendium of the work, of which we will soon have occasion to speak [2].

In the MS., after a letter and an introduction by Theo-

1) Add. (Rich) 7,189. Cf. the Cat. of Rosen and Forshall, p. 74.

2) Cf. Wright's remarks, supplementary to the Cat. of R. and F., at the close of vol. III of his Catalogue.

dosios, and immediately preceding the introductory chapter of the text, is a short preface or rather dedication by the person, real or supposititious, who translated the work from Greek into Syriac: it is addressed to his Maecenas, a certain ܦܝܠܝܘܣ „Philios", at whose request he undertook the work. Theodosios appends a commentary to this dedication in the same manner as he does to the text of the work itself: in no case could he have been the author of the translation. The same anonymous translator also adds a postscript at the end of the volume, addressed to the same Philios, in which he speaks of completing and sending him his translation, with an accompanying letter.

The Syriac itself is remarkably idiomatic, pure and easy, and shows no trace of being fettered by the necessities of a translation: this is very evident in comparison with the Syriac translation of Dionysios, in which the strained and unidiomatic character of the language is apparent at every point, though it is the work of such an able man as Sergios of Ras'ain.

If the Book of Hierotheos be considered the work of Bar Sudaili, two hypotheses naturally present themselves for the explanation of the linguistic purity we have mentioned. 1) We may allow that Bar Sudaili wrote the work in Greek, but that, in order to foster his propaganda in the region of Edessa, he translated it himself into Syriac: or 2) we may suppose that the existence of a Greek original is purely fictitious, and that the Syriac text we possess is the real original. This fiction of a Greek text was necessary to render the imposture credible, because, if genuine, the Book of Hierotheos must have been written in Greek. In this case the pretended translator's introduction and note were a fiction of Bar Sudaili along with the text, and we would not need to be surprised at the non-appearance of the supposed Greek original. This latter supposition seems the most plausible, after a careful study of the text: the only valid objection would be the existence of any traces of a Greek text. I have found an apparent one, but its value is so questionable that it can hardly weigh in the balance. In a Latin catalogue of Greek MSS. existing at Constantinople towards 1600 we find the following title [1]): "Explicatio S. Cyrilli Arciepiscopi Alexandriae in S. Hierotheum Areopagitam." There are two objections to this being a reliable proof. 1) This work of Cyril is necessarily an imposture, as he lived more than a half-century before Bar Sudaili and Pseudo-Dionysios, and consequently it may have been written by some monk, a follower of Bar Sudaili's doctrine, as an additional prop to the stage-work of his fiction. 2) There seems to have existed some confusion between the persons of Hierotheos and Dionysios; in evidence of which we will give a passage from Pseudo-Dionysios quoted in an early Syriac MS. (IX century) as by Hierotheos [2]), and furthermore in this

---

1) Antonii Possevini, Apparatus Sacer. Coloniae Agrippinae 1608. T. II; in fine, p. 46, under the heading: »Ex catalogo Librorum variis in locis Constantinopoli extantium, qui sunt graece MS. quique a Grammatico fuere exhibiti.

2) Brit. Mus. Add. 17,191 (of IX or X cent.) f. 64: ܕܒܝܕܝܫܐ ܐܝܪܬܐܘܣ. ܡܢ ܬܫܒܘܚܬܗ: ܕܐܦܠܐ ܕܝܢ ܠܩܕ̈ܝܫܐ ܐܬܘܗܝ، ܦܓܪܐ ܠܘܬ ܚܙܬܐ. ܠܗܢܐ ܗܘ. ܡܢ ܗ̇، ܕܐܦ ܒܪ ܐܬܘܗܝ ܕܠܐ ܦܓܪܐ. ܡܚܝܢܐ ܕܐܘܩܝܢܐ ܒܚܫܟܬܐ. ܐܚܘܢܐ ܕܐܡܬܘܪܝܢ ܐܦ ܠܐ ܬ̈ܪܝܢ. ܗܝܕܝܢ ܘܒܬܫܒ̈ܚܬܐ ܘܒܩܕ̈ܝܫܘܬܐ ܘܒܦܓܪܐ: ܗܘܝܐ ܐܬܘܗܝ ܒܚܫܟܬܐ. ܒܫܠܡܘܬܐ ܘܡܫܠܡܢܘܬܐ ܕܡܢ ܘܠܒܐ ܕܠܡܫܡܫܢܘ ... This passage is in reality from *Divine Names*, ch.

same catalogue of Constantinople MSS. we read the title: "Liber sancti Hierothei, sive Dionysii Areopagitae, Episcopi Atheniensis Theologicus, Hierarchia, et Mystica Theologia"[1]). Here the confusion is evident, and the reason for it is patent: both were legendary personages, both supposed to have been members of the Areopagos, disciples of S. Paul, bishops of Athens, and to have lived in Spain. It is then quite natural to suppose that this Pseudo-Cyrillian commentary may after all have treated of the Pseudo-Dionysian writings. In confirmation of this we may refer to the fact that at the council of Constantinople in 532, when the Dionysian writings were first brought forward, their supporters alleged that S. Cyril had quoted them: this fact was disputed by the orthodox, and the quarrel became quite warm.

We have already noticed the great difficulty experienced by Bar 'Ebraia in procuring a copy of the Book of Hierotheos; but it is at first surprising to find that the patriarch Theodosios and his friend Lazaros, bishop of Kyros, experienced the same difficulty nearly four centuries before him: both of them were most desirous of becoming acquainted with the work, of taking it as their guide, and of unfolding its mysteries; and, as Theodosios informs us in his letter to his friend Lazaros, they finally succeeded. Our surprise, however, ceases when we read the opening chapters of the book itself, and perceive the frank and bold clearness with which the author develops his anti-christian and ultra-pantheistic system. That he is conscious, all the time, of the

---

IV, § 27. Ὅτι δὲ οὐδὲ κακίας αἴτιον τῇ ψυχῇ τὸ σῶμα, δῆλον ἐκ τοῦ δυνατὸν εἶναι καὶ ἄνευ σώματος παρυφίστασθαι κακίαν, ὥσπερ ἐν δαίμοσι· τοῦτο γάρ ἐστι καὶ νοῖς, καὶ ψυχαῖς, καὶ σώμασι κακὸν, ἡ τῆς ἕξεως τῶν οἰκείων ἀγαθῶν ἀσθένεια καὶ ἀπόπτωσις.

1) Ant. Possevini, ibid.

peril he runs, is evident from the oft-repeated injunction, under the severest penalties, not to disclose the mysteries of the book before "impure minds" (i. e. orthodox). Both the pretended Syrian translator in his introduction, and Theodosios in his commentary, reiterate this caution most emphatically. This secrecy is the keynote to the method of teaching of the Book of Hierotheos, and the assurance that the doctrines would not pass beyond the circle of the initiated explains the boldness of the language. We now see not only the reason for the scarcity of copies and for the difficulty in obtaining one, but also why the book occupied so exceptional a position.

We could hardly expect to find any general acquaintance with a work the knowledge and use of which was kept confined as much as possible to the narrow circle of esoteric mystics: even if inimical hands, attracted by vague reports, sought to obtain possession of it, they must have been generally baffled by the discretion and secrecy of the initiated, who were familiar with the anathemas launched against all disclosers of its mystical doctrines. Theodosios himself, however, leads us to conclude that before his time a number of theologians had commentated the work, but he omits to mention any of them by name. It is possible that he refers, among others, to Kyriakos and John of Dara, whom we have already quoted. This is all the more probable, because he speaks of these theologians as objecting to Hierotheos' doctrine of the redemption of the hell-sphere, which is precisely what Kyriakos and John of Dara do.

IX.

THE POSITION GIVEN TO HIEROTHEOS BY PSEUDO-DIONYSIOS.

Turning to other writings which relate to our book, we must pause to consider the position given by Pseudo-Dionysios to his master Hierotheos: we have already alluded to the terms of great reverence and admiration which he uses with regard to him. The portrait he gives of Hierotheos tallies completely with what we know of Bar Sudaili: the mysticism, the celestial visions, the abstruse and condensed thought, the study of Scripture. I will here translate the chapter in which Pseudo-Dionysios explains his relations to his master [1]). „And here it is suitable to explain wherefore, inasmuch as our illustrious master Hierotheos has made an admirable collection of 'Theological Elements', we have, as if these were not sufficient, written others beside the present theological treatise. Certainly, had he claimed to write, systematically, treatises on all theological questions, and had in special expositions developed the sum of all theology, we would never have had the folly or the stupidity to consider ourselves better able than he to treat of theological matters in a clear and divine manner; or to talk at random, by repeating the same things super-

1) Divine Names, ch. III, 2—3.

fluously; and moreover show ourselves unjust towards a teacher and friend by whom, after S. Paul, we were instructed, by plagiarizing his most excellent doctrine and expositions. But since he, in reality explaining divine things in a way suited to mature minds, enounced unto us certain synoptic statements, which in one included many, he as it were encouraged me and others, who like myself are teachers of newly-initiated souls, to unfold and interpret, in a language suited to us, the synoptic and universal meditations of the spiritual power of so great a man. Thou [1]) hast often thyself urged me to do so, and didst return to me his book as being too sublime. Therefore do we assign this teacher of perfect and mature intelligences unto those who are above the crowd, as second Scriptures, analogous to those divinely inspired. We however will transmit divine things to those like us in a manner suited to us. For, if solid food is for the perfect, what supreme perfection must it be to furnish such to others? Therefore have we truly said that the direct vision of spiritual truths and their synoptic teaching require a mature power, but that the acquaintance with and understanding of the truths leading up to them is suited to the inferior consecrators and priests. However, this has been most carefully observed by us, never to take in hand the things which this divine teacher has explained with sufficient clearness, lest we fall into tautology by giving the same explanation of a passage which he has already cited. For among our divinely-inspired hierarchs (when we, as thou knowest, together with him and many of our holy brothers had come together for the contemplation of the life-giving and God-receiving body, when James the brother of God, and Peter the supreme and

---

1) Timothy, to whom the *Divine Names* is addressed.

venerable chief of theologians were present, it was decided, after the contemplation, that all the hierarchs should sing hymns, as each one was able, to the all powerful goodness of the thearchic infirmity) as you know, he excelled, after the theologians, all other initiated, being entirely beside himself, all in an ecstasy, and feeling communion with that which he was praising in hymns. He was considered by all those who heard and saw him, whether they knew him or not, to be divinely inspired and a divine psalmist. But wherefore should I speak to you of the divine things which were there said: for, unless my memory betrays me, I feel certain that I have often heard from you fragments of these divinely enthusiastic psalmodies, such zeal did you feel in searching diligently after divine things.

"But, passing over these mysteries, both because they are not be mentioned to the common crowd and because they are well-known to you, when it was necessary to confer with the multitude and to draw as many as possible to our own holy doctrine, how he surpassed the greater part of sacred teachers, in the use of time, in purity of mind, in acuteness of demonstration, and the rest of sacred discourses, so that we did not attempt even to look such a great light (lit. sun) in the face! For we are conscious and aware of not being sufficiently able either to comprehend those divine things which are intelligible, or to express and explain those divines doctrines which are expressible; being left so far behind by the knowledge of these divine men in theological truth, that through excessive timidity we would have even concluded not to hear or say anything on divine philosophy, had we not perceived that it was not right to neglect what it is possible for us to know of divine things. We were persuaded of this not only by the natural aspirations of intelligences always filled with the desire for the contemplation, in so far as is allowed, of supernatural things, but also by the very excellent disposition of the divine ordinances, which while it forbids to meddle with what is above us, both as being superior to our worth and as unattainable, yet bids us to learn with zeal whatever is allowed and given to us, urging us to communicate generously to others. Persuaded then by this, and not desisting or shrinking from that search after divine things which is within our reach, and not bearing patiently that those who are not able to contemplate the things above us should remain without help, we have undertaken to write, not pretending to teach anything new, but interpreting and showing forth, by investigations more minute and applied to distinct parts, what had been said synoptically by Hierotheos". In another place (Div. Names II, 9) Dionysios says, as a preface to his quotation from Hierotheos' Elements of Theology: "this has been unfolded in a supernatural manner by our illustrious teacher in his Elements of Theology, which he in part received from pious theologians, in part conceived by a scientific investigation of Scripture through his frequent exercise and practice therein, and in part was taught by some more divine inspiration, by not only learning but experiencing divine things (*οὐ μόνον μαθὼν, ἀλλὰ καὶ παθὼν τὰ θεῖα*) and by his sympathy (*συμπαθείας*) with them, if we may so express ourselves, made perfect in the unteachable and mystical union with and faith in them".

The text of the quotations from Hierotheos will be given with the text of the Book of Hierotheos for the sake of comparison. They have already been referred to on p. 6.

In regard to these fragments it will not be out of place

to refer to an error committed by Dorner [1]). He makes an elaborate statement of the Christology of Pseudo-Dionysios, and founds it entirely on the quotations from Hierotheos' "Elements of Theology" in the Divine Names. All his conclusions must simply be transferred to Hierotheos. This is important, because the language of Dionysios himself concerning Christ is in quite a different form and in thought more theological, while that of his master is ontological and mystical. We seek in vain in the Book of Hierotheos for any of the quotations given in the "Divine Names"; but, as we have remarked, this could be no argument against the identification of Hierotheos with Bar Sudaili, for in no case would it have been prudent for Stephen's disciple to give passages from a work which the sect desired to keep as secret as possible.

We find perhaps the earliest mention of Hierotheos, after the appearance of the Dionysian writings, in the almost contemporary history of Zacharias Rhetor. This historian, in giving a portrait of the famous Severos of Antioch, describes him as "learned in the Holy Scriptures, and in the commentaries on them by ancient writers, by *Hïerotheos* and Dionysios, Titus and Timothy, disciples of the apostles; and after them by Ignatios, Clement, and Irenaios, etc." [2]). It would seem probable that Zacharias, who, it must be added, was himself quite a religious philosopher, points to something more being known, of the writings which passed under the name of Hierotheos, than the few fragments given by Pseudo-Dionysios. This passage would then be interesting, as it would show that Severos, who was a supporter of

---

1) History of the doctrine of the Person of Christ, D. II, v. I. p. 157 sqq.
2) Land, Anecdota Syriaca T. III, p. 228.

Dionysian doctrines, favored also those of Pseudo-Hierotheos. Were the writings of Severos better known, more light might be thrown on the subject of his relation to the mystical school.

We have already mentioned the spurious "Explicatio S. Cyrilli" on Hierotheos, and the probable confusion between Dionysios and his master: in this connection it may be remarked that it has been already suggested by the learned Dailly [1]) that the Hierotheos spoken of by Pseudo-Dionysios is none but the latter himself, for in his opinion Hierotheos was an invented name. It is likely that this explanation may have suggested itself from the entire lack of information at that time regarding any person of this name or any works written by or attributed to him, with the single exception of what we read in Pseudo-Dionysios.

It would seem impossible for any one, after reading even an outline of the Book of Hierotheos, to accept for a moment this theory of identification. The intellectual position of the two minds is entirely different: Pseudo-Hierotheos is a simple monk, whose thought is entirely distinct from any philosophic system, claiming direct vision, drawing his theories from his own consciousness, and expressing them with great naïveté and freshness; it is the divine seer, and not the philosophic genius, who speaks. On reading his book one feels it to be the genuine out-pouring of a strongly-excited religious imagination, and the work of an original mind, but of no eclectic or imitator. It is true we find in his system ideas from both the Christian and pagan schools of Alexandria — especially from Origen — as well as traces

---

1) Joannes Dallæus, De scriptis quae Dionysii Areopagitæ et Ignatii Antiocheni nominibus circumferuntur. Geneva 1666.

of the kabbalistic and gnostic systems and perhaps even of the early Chaldaean cosmogony: but they are marshalled into a perfectly symmetrical and harmonious whole, in subordination to the ideal peculiar to Hierotheos himself. With him there is never any attempt at discussion. His theories are successively unfolded as absolute and undeniable certainties, as revelations, as things which he has known and seen.

On the other hand, although Pseudo-Dionysios shows much of the same spirit in his Mystical Theology and Divine Names, yet even here there appears the logical element so conspicuous in his writings, which classifies him in a different branch of the mystical school from that of Pseudo-Hierotheos, as well as in far closer connection with the Neo-Platonists. We might say, that the one has a considerable affinity with the West-Syrian school of Antioch, and that the other belongs to the East-Syrian school of Edessa: for these represented, the former, the intellectual and logical side of the Syrian development, and the latter, its sentimental, symbolical and analogical side.

X.

THE QUESTION OF THE PRIORITY OF HIEROTHEOS TO DIONYSIOS.

This leads to the discussion of another question, which may already have occurred to the reader. Is it not natural to suppose that the Book of Hierotheos was produced precisely in view of the references to Hierotheos in Pseudo-Dionysios, and is dependent on the latter, and consequently of no independent value? Would it not have been quite possible that a follower of Dionysios should have fancied to sustain his master's position by bringing out a work which should bear out his relation to Hierotheos? Were this the case, the author of a work of this kind would naturally have made it to correspond with the indications in Dionysios: would in all likelihood have entitled his work the ***Θεολογικαὶ Στοιχειώσεις*** or Principles of Theology, and with it would have incorporated, as a proof of authenticity, the passages quoted from that book in the Divine Names. He would also have referred more than once by name to his beloved disciple Dionysios. Supposing it to be an artificial production of this kind, would it not also be natural to find it a work entirely imitative, in the same style of thought as the Dionysian writings, but lacking their power and originality?

Now we find nothing of all this in the Book of Hierotheos: not only is the title different, and does it treat necessarily of a different order of ideas — the ontological and cosmological — but there is no sign of the passages quoted by Dionysios. Even the name of Dionysios is not mentioned, though the work seems to be dedicated to him: he is only referred to as "my son" or "my friend" [1]). There is throughout no trace of any attempt to connect itself with the Pseudo-Dionysian writings. Besides this, what has already been noted regarding the difference in intellectual standpoint, style and form of thought is sufficient, I think, to preclude the idea of imitation: for it is clear that the relation in which the two stand to each other as presenting, the one, sentimental and analogical forms, and the other, intellectual and logical forms of the same ideas, gives, according to the natural development of schools, the priority to Hierotheos.

In this relation, reference must be made to a very sagacious conjecture made by Dorner, which is all the more remarkable because he had such meagre materials at hand on which to base it. He says: "Hierotheus was professedly the teacher of Dionysius; and under the name of Hierotheus Barsudaili wrote the work in which he taught the transition of all things into the divine nature. Such is the account given by Barhebraeus. Among the Monophysites the writings of the Areopagite were much used, translated and commentated. It is possible that Barsudaili's fiction, — a fiction to which he may have been led by the Origenism which prevailed in many of the monasteries, and which formed a bridge to Neo-Platonism, — *may have given rise to the spread of Neo-Platonism in a Church form, under the name*

---

1) S. Paul is spoken of by name as his master.

of the holy disciple of Hierotheus" [1]). In this passage Dorner recognizes the true relation between the two writers, and this position of his is now amply confirmed. Gfrörer also in his Church History draws similar conclusions in his remarks on the Pseudo-Dionysian writings. Who was Pseudo-Dionysios? In his opinion a follower of Proklos, and by birth a Syrian. This latter position he attempts to prove by the relations between Dionysios and Hierotheos.

Taking then for granted the priority of Hierotheos, is it not singular that Dionysios should not have mentioned this most important work of his master? As we have already explained, this silence was necessary to the preservation of the secret character of the book.

A comparison of dates does not throw any difficulties in the way of the priority of Hierotheos. Bar Sudaili we know to have flourished during the last decade of the fifth century and the beginning of the sixth, while the first signs of the appearance of the Pseudo-Dionysian writings occur probably during the second decade of the sixth century at the earliest, the first certain date being that of the Council of 532—33. That they were already known before this date of 532 seems certain, and Sergios' Syriac version was probably slightly anterior.

---

1) Dorner, J. A., History of development of the doctrine of the Person of Christ. Edinb. 1861. D. II. v. I. p. 422—23.

XI.

COMMENTARIES ON THE BOOK OF HIEROTHEOS.

To return to the Syrian writers who have treated this book in extenso, we find still remaining to us two works of importance: the first is the commentary of Theodosios of Antioch, and the second is an abridgment of the work by Gregory Bar ʿEbraia. These two are of very unequal value, for the latter is more an imitation than a work of any original merit.

The physician Romanos, on becoming Jacobite Patriarch of Antioch in 887, took the name of Theodosios: his two great works seem to have been his commentary on Hierotheos and a treatise on medicine 1). He must have been an enthusiastic follower of the mystico-pantheistic school, as also his friend Lazaros of Kyros at whose request he undertook and to whom he dedicated his work. The letter which he addresses to Lazaros at the beginning of his commentary would be of great interest: unfortunately the first sheets of the MS. are so defaced that but a small portion of it can be satisfactorily deciphered. In it he recounts how both he

---

1) H. Zotenberg, Les sentences symboliques de Théodose, patriarche d'Antioche. Paris 1877, p. 8—9.

and his friends desired to procure a copy of the Book of Hierotheos in order that it should become their leader on the way of salvation. It is a significant fact that the highest dignitaries of the Syrian Church should adopt as their esoteric Bible, so to speak, as a divine revelation, a work like this. A few passages from this letter will be given in a note, to illustrate what has just been said and to show the reasons which led Theodosios to undertake his commentary [1]).

---

1) ...... ܠܦܛܪܝܪܟܐ ܩܕܝܫܐ ܘܪܘܚܢܐ. ܘܡܕܒܪܢܘܬܗ ܕܒܪܝܬܐ ܕܩܕܝܫܐ ܐܢܛܝܘܟܝܐ. ܣܦܩܬ ܐܢܐ ܠܡܟܬܒ ܠܟ: ܟܕ ܐܢܬ ܡܢ ܠܒܘܬܗ ܕܢܦܫܟ ܬܟܬܒ ܠܗ ܠܦܛܪܝܪܟܐ ܗܢܐ ܩܕܝܫܐ ܘܐܠܗܝܐ. ܟܕ ܠܐ ܫܠܝܢ ܘܠܐܬܘܬܐ ܒܟܠܐ ܕܐܦܘܕܝܢ ܕܟܬܪ ܫܬܘܬܗ ܕܗܢܐ ܟܬܒܐ. ܘܐܦܠܐ ܐܬܚܫܒܬ ܟܠܝܢ ܠܫܘܬܗ ܘܐܦ ܟܠܠܬܐ ܕܠܐ ܒܥܒܕ ܗܘܬ ܠܝ. ܕܣܘܪܗܒ ܬܫܡܫܬܐ ܡܫܡܫ ܕܗܠܝܢ ܕܒܠܥܐ. ܐܦܠܐ ܐܢܐ ܡܨܝܬ ܕܐܚܠܝܢ ܡܢ ܗܢܐ ܡܘܬܪܐ. ܘܐܦ ܬܚܘܝܬܐ ܕܡܠܐ ܐܬܘܬܗ. ܐܠܐ ܘܡܘܗܪܐ ܕܬܘܪ ܥܒܝܕ ܢܣܒܝܢ ܡܢܗ: ܘܐܦ ܐܝܟ ܕܒܡܘܬܐ ܕܪܘܚܐ ܣܥܒ ܐܢܬ ܠܝ. ܗܿܝ ܕܗܒܐܪܐ ܣܠܡ ܕܡܢܐ ܘܠܒܝܐ: ܐܠܐ ܘܡܛܠ ܕܐܝܟ ܕܡܘܬܪܬܐ ܙܥܘܪܐ ܟܠܗ ܕܡܢܝ ܠܬܘܪܥܐ ܕܐܝܟ ܗܢܐ ܙܥܘܪܐ ܘܕܡܡ ܟܠܕܘܟ ܡܬܥܢܝ. ܗܢܐ ܙܥܘܪܐ ܠܗ ܕܐܦ ܐܬܠ. ܗܢܐ ܗܢܠ ܕܢܐ ܠܗ ܬܪܥܝܬܐ. ܕܐܡܬܐ ܕܙܥܘܪܐ ܟܠ ܘܪܒܐ ܐܢܐ ܠܡܐܣܒ. ܗܢܐ ܬܘܒ ܒܐܢܐ ܘܣܒܒܐ. ܗܿܝ ܕܢܬܠ. ܐܢܫܘ ܗܿܢ ܕܫܡܫܐܝܬ ܪܒܐ ܐܢܐ ܠܡܬܪܕ ܒܐܘܪܚܐ ܕܐܠܗܐ. ܡܢ ܢܡܘܣܐ ܕܐܠܗܐ ܢܒܥ ܕܢܗ ܒܠܒܢ. ܐܝܟ ܗܿܝ ܕܐܡܪܢܐ ܕܒܒܢ ܕܒܠܒܢ ܗܢܐ ܠܡܥܢܝܢ ܠܐ ܬܒܥܐ.

Immediately following the letter is a long introduction by Theodosios, in which he summarizes the book, explains his view of it, and enters into an elaborate and interesting interpretation of all the mystical and philosophical terms used in the text — interpretations which are valuable not only for the understanding of the work, but often also philologically.

The commentary of Theodosios is very detailed, and occupies about three-quarters of the 4to volume of 134 pages. He is very careful to define and explain all the expressions used, and often does so in a very mystical and fanciful manner. In his opinion, the most abstruse doctrines in the book are veiled under words which would suffice to hide them from the uninitiated, but to "pure minds" "be easy of interpretation."

ܠܐ ܓܝܪ ܐܝܬ ܠܝ ܗ̇ܘ ܗܢܐ ܕܐܢܟܬ ܠܟ ܡܢܗ. ܡܦܣ ܐܢܐ
ܕܝܢ ܒܡܠܝܢ ܐܦ ܒܗ̇ ܒܡܫܠܡܘܬܟ ܡܛܪ ܐܢܐ. ܐܠܐ ܘܡܛܠ
ܕܠܬܒܐ ܗܢܐ ܐܝܟ ܕܠܘܬ ܒܢ̈ܝ ܥܕܬܐ ܕܗܝܡܢܘܬܐ. ܘܠܘܬ
ܐܝܠܝܢ ܕܡܫܡܫܝܢ ܠܐܪ̈ܙܐ ܐܬܟܬܒ. ܐܦ ܗܢܐ ܗܘܐ ܗܫܐ ܠܘܬܟ
ܦܫ .... ܘܡܛܠ ܗܕܐ ܐܫܬܕܪܬ ܠܦܘܪܫܢ ܕܠܬܒܐ ܗܢܐ
ܡܕܥܐ ܐܦܫܡ. ܠܘ ܐܝܟ ܙ̈ܪܐ ܕܒܥܝܢ ܒܗ ܗܕܐ ܡܥܒܕ
ܐܢܐ. ܐܠܐ ܐܡܟܢܐ ܕܗܘܦܟܐ ܒܫܠܡܘܬܟ ܠܘܬ ܗܕܐ
ܡܬܬܪܝܒ ܐܢܐ ∴ .... »the holy and mystical doctrine, hidden in allegories, of the blessed Hierotheos. I will endeavor to interpret to you, as you in the goodness of your heart have asked, this holy and divine teaching. For the labors and fatigue in searching after this book never discouraged you, neither were you stopped by the lack of it, nor by the pains you were obliged to take to remove the veil from off the words of the Teacher. I do not therefore wish to defraud you of this profit. Even if it is a laborious work, yet will we derive from it a most glorious illumination.» etc. etc.

Besides the general introduction, each one of the five books is preceded by a particular one. To the text of the chapters the commentary is attached in two different ways in different parts of the MS.: either the whole chapter of the text is first given, and then repeated in short sections, each with a separate commentary; or else, in order to avoid repetition, the latter system alone is used without first giving the whole text. As a scientific, thorough and systematic work, this commentary is remarkable, and gives a favorable idea of the possibilities of Syrian learning.

There is nothing in any part of Theodosios' writings to indicate that he did not believe implicitly in the authorship of a genuine first-century Hierotheos: we will soon have to refer to the probable sincerity of this belief.

Bar ʿEbraia also interested himself in the Book of Hierotheos, and sent emissaries throughout the East to procure a copy: he finally obtained one, which, strange to say, is the identical copy now preserved in the British Museum [1]), and that to which we are indebted for our knowledge of the work. From this MS. he drew up a compendium, to which he added a running commentary, derived principally from that of Theodosios. He took however great liberties with the text, and showed the true unscrupulousness of an Eastern in distorting it for the purpose of softening its anti-christian tone and hiding its real character [2]). The worst part of the process to which he submitted the book was the entire change he made in the order of the chapters, placing near

1) See the note on the last page of the MS., where the fact is noticed and an account of the search is given. Cf. Wright's Cat. vol. III, supplem.

2) Ms. copies of this work exist in Paris (Bib. Nat. Fonds Syr. 227), in Oxford, and in the British Museum (Syr. MS. 850; Wright, Cat. p. 893 and Add. 1017).

each other those which belonged to the beginning and end, and uniting in one others which had not the slightest relation. As we have already remarked that, in the Book of Hierotheos, all the parts are mutually dependent, it may well be imagined that the compendium of Bar ʿEbraia, being made in this manner, is devoid of all order and rational sense, and gives no idea of the scope of the original. The excuse he gives in his introduction is, that he found the primitive order to have been inverted and the text corrupted by the translator![1]).

---

1) ܗܕܝܢ ܐܘ̄ ܐܚܘܢ ܪܘܚܢܝܐ ܗܕܐ ܕܒܢܐ ܣܘܟܠܐ ܗܘܪܟܬ
ܘܐܬܬܣܝܡܬ ܒܟܬܒܐ ܕܫܡܝܢܝܐ ܘܡܕܡܝܢܘܬܐ ܡܫܒܚܐ
ܐܝܪܐܬܐܘܣ. ܚܙܝܬܗ ܠܟܬܒܐ ܗܢܐ ܘܡܫܚܠܦܐ. ܒܬܪ ܚܢܐ
ܐܝܟ ܠܡܐܡܪ̈ܘܗܝ ܘܠܦܣܘܩܐܘܗܝ ܫ̈ܠܝܛܐ ܘܐܪ̈ܟܝܐ ܘܩ̈ܠܝܠܐ.
ܘܡܨܠܘܬ ܠܡܕܡ ܡܢ ܦܬܓܡ̈ܘܗܝ. ܘܗܕܐ ܠܗ ܡܢܗ ܡܢ
ܡܬܬܒܥܐ ܒܗܕܐ. ܐܠܐ ܡܢ ܡܫܒܠܢܐ. ܒܠܚܘܕ ܘܡܠܗ ܕܡܢ
ܡܘܕܝܢܐ ܠܡܦܪܫܢܐ. ܘܗܘܐ ܠܝ ܫܘܥܒܕܐ ܡܕܡ ܕܢܦܠܓܗ
ܐܝܟ ܘܦܫܩ ܠܟܠ ܚܕ ܚܕ ܒܕܘܟܬܐ ܕܗܘܝܐ ܠܗ ܘܐܫܟܚܐ
ܕܢܣܒ ܠܗ ܐܝܟ ܪܚܝܡ. ܘܐܝܟ ܡܐ ܕܡܫܒܪܝܢ. ܘܟܕ ܒܒܕܝܢ
ܗܕܐ ܠܐ ܒܠܒܠܝܢ ܠܟ̈ܠܗܘܢ ܕܒܘܟܪܝܐ. ܘܐܦܠܐ ܠܟ̈ܠܗܘܢ
ܕܡܦܫܩܢܐ ܒܐܘܪܚܬ ܠܐ ܚܫܠܦܝܢ ܐܘ ܐܘܣܦܝܢ ܡܢ ܡܕܡ.
ܐܠܐ ܐ̄ܘ ܒܬܪ ܩ̈ܠܐ ܒܢܣ̈ܐ. ܐܝܟ ܟܕ ܘܕܝܢ ܘܐܦ.
ܘܡܕܡ ܕܕܡܝܐ ܠܗܠܝܢ ܒܠܚܘܕ. ܒܬܪ ܐܘܟܝܢ ܡܢܗܘܢ ܠܡܕܡ
ܕܐܬܝܗ̈ܘܢ، ܒܝܬ ܡܬܪܢܐ. ܘܐܝܟ ܩ̈ܠܝܠܐ ܘܦܣܘ̈ܩܐ ܡܕܡ
ܡܬܩ̈ܢܢܐ. ܘܐܝܟ ܡܠ̈ܦܢܐ ܕܐܣܛܪܘܠܘܓܝܐ ܘܡܕܡ ܕܕܡܐ
ܠܗܘܢ. ܘܐܦ ܗܘܐ ܒܗ ܦܬܓ̈ܡܐ ܡܕܡ ܡܫ̈ܦܪܢܐ
ܒܕܘܟܬܐ ܡܫܬܠܡܬܐ ܕܠܗܘܢ ܒܚܘܒܢ. ܒܬܪ ܗܫܟܝܢ ܬܘܒ

It is a singular circumstance that Bar ʿEbraia, who, as we have seen, states emphatically in other places that Bar Sudaili was the real author, does not mention or even insinuate the fact in this compendium or in his introduction to it, but on the contrary speaks of the work as genuine.

It is perhaps possible that his inimical position to the Book of Hierotheos dated from an earlier period, when as yet he had not laid eyes on it and found it so much to his taste. If this were so, he had obvious reasons for not laying any stress on its authorship by the anathematized Bar Sudaili. This raises, however, another important question: did Theodosios know that Bar Sudaili was the author, or even that the work was attributed to him? I do not consider his complete silence on the question, and his open acceptance of the authenticity, to be a sound proof of his good faith in considering the work as that of a first-century Hierotheos.

ܠܡܦܩܢܘܬܐ ܕܟܬܒܐ ܗܢܐ ܥܠ ܡܬܪܓܡܢܘܬܗ ܕܥܒܪܝ.

ܕܥ. ܐܚܝ ܪܘܚܢܝܐ ܠܟ ܡܢ ܙܒܢܐ ܣܓܝ ܘܟ »Know, my spiritual brother, that having for a long time studied and considered the Book of the illustrious, wise and learned Hierotheos, I have found it to be a great and wonderful book: but I perceived that its books and chapters were confused, lengthened and corrupted, as also were some of its sentences, and that this had been done not by the above-mentioned writer but by the translator. I therefore desired to translate it from Greek into Syriac, and decided also to put (its chapters) in order, and to arrange each one in the place it ought to occupy and to which, *in our judgment and opinion*, it was suited. In doing this, however, we have not corrupted the words of the learned (author) nor the words of the commentator, not having changed or added any thing of our own except only a few words, such as ܕܝܢ and ܕܐܦ and ܐܦ and other similar ones. Still we have removed some things of small importance, as well as some *perverted chapters and sections*; and things like the theory of astrology, although there were perverse sentences in many places which agreed with it. We have arranged the chapters of this book according to the economy of the life of Our Lord, beginning with his baptism," etc. etc.

We have seen it to be a fact well known in the Syrian literary and religious world of that period, that the Book was attributed to Stephen. Now of this fact such a man as Theodosios could not have been ignorant when it was well known to Kyriakos and John of Dara. But it would have been quite natural for him to repudiate and conceal such knowledge; for even at that time it would have been regarded as a very questionable step for the leaders of the Church to take, as their spiritual guide, an openly-reprobated pantheist.

XII.

SUMMARY OF THE BOOK OF HIEROTHEOS ON THE HIDDEN MYSTERIES OF THE DIVINITY.

It would not be possible within the limits of a few pages to give a satisfactory summary of a work written in such a condensed style, and full of so many unusual, and to us strange, ideas: still we will endeavor to give, as far as possible, a correct idea of the work, using, if not the exact wording of the author, a very similar language. We have purposely avoided attempting a critical analysis, or a comparison with earlier writings which contain similar doctrines; all this can be done only when we publish the text itself.

The full title of the work is not given on the first sheet of the MS., but appears from the introductory commentary to be ܟܬܒܐ ܕܩܕܝܫܐ ܐܝܪܘܬܐܘܣ: ܕܥܠ ܐܪ̈ܙܐ ܟܣ̈ܝܐ ܕܒܝܬ ܐܠܗܐ. *The Book of the holy Hierotheos on the hidden mysteries of the Divinity* (lit. of the house of God). It is divided into five books, each of which contains a number of chapters. It is a real theological epic, in which the mystical scenes through which the soul passes in its ascent towards the One are developed in a vivid manner, as if the writer saw "heaven open and the angels of God ascending and descending upon the Son of man". The writer himself professes to have more than once attained to the highest point of mystic union with the Arch-Good.

To describe the contents in a few words: at the beginning we find the statement regarding absolute existence, and the emanation from primordial essence of the spiritual and material universes: then comes, what occupies almost the entire work, the experience of the mind in search of perfection during this life. Finally comes the description of the various phases of existence as the mind rises into complete union with and ultimate absorption into the primitive essence. The key-note to the experience of the mind is its absolute identification with Christ; but the Son finally resigns the kingdom unto the Father, and all distinct existence comes to an end, being lost in the chaos of the Good.

BOOK FIRST.

Every intelligent nature is determined, known and comprehended by the essence which is above it; and determines, knows and comprehends the essence which is below it; but to the pure mind alone belongs the vision above and below [1]). Not even to the intelligence of angels are the wonderful mysteries of pure and holy minds revealed.

---

1) In Hierotheos the Arch-Good (ܪܫܝܬ ܛܒܘܬܐ, ܛܒܘܬܐ ܡܫܒܚܬܐ) is the first, indefinite and all-embracing principle. The Universal Essence (ܐܘܣܝܐ ܕܟܠ), the Unity, or the Neo-Platonic One, is second in order of emanation: it contains within itself the principles of distinction (see p. 95), and does not appear to be different from what is termed the first fall out of the Good.

The Good, which we glorify, is the universal constituting, providing, and sustaining power of the Universe; *from which* all distinct existences came to be through separation, *by which* their being is sustained, and *to which* they constantly desire to return.

Distinctions were established from the Universal Essence in this wise. The Good being uniform could not produce anything not uniform: therefore, when the fall from the Good took place, distinct orders of existence did not immediately come into being, *for uniformity cannot produce distinction:* on the contrary, *distinction comes from the distinct orders of the Divine Nature, from all the distinct and unequal natures of man, and of the animals that crawl upon the earth, and of birds and of beasts and of fishes, and also of the distinct beings that are under the earth, and those which suffer many torments in hell* [1]). Unto all these *the measure of their descent from the Good determines the extent of their fall* [2]). *When the fall from the Good happened to all things at once, a quiet and silence extended itself over all: they were then like that which is not* [3]): *perhaps they possessed*

---

1) ܕܐܝܬܘܬܗܘܢ ܕܝܢ ܦܘܪܫܢܐ ܡܢ ܠܚܡ̈ܫܐ ܦܪ̈ܝܫܐ ܕܟܝܢܬ ܐܠܗܐ܆ ܡܢܝܢ ܠܡܥܒܕ. ܘܡܢ ܟ̈ܝܢܐ ܟܠܗܘܢ ܦܪ̈ܝܫܐ ܘܠܐ ܫ̈ܘܝܐ ܕܐܢܫܐ ܘܕܪ̈ܚܫܬܐ ܕܪ̈ܚܫܝܢ ܥܠ ܐܪܥܐ܆ ܘܕܦ̈ܪܚܬܐ ܘܕܒܥܝܪܐ ܘܕܢܘ̈ܢܐ܆ ܘܕܐܘܣܝ̈ܣ ܬܘܒ ܡܫ̈ܚܠܦܬܐ ܘܦܪ̈ܝܫܬܐ ܘܕܠܬܚܬ ܡܢ ܐܪܥܐ܆ ܘܕܐܝܠܝܢ ܕܒܫܝ̈ܘܠ ܡܫܢ̈ܩܬܐ ܡܫܬܢܩܝܢ܀

2) ܡܫܘܠܬܐ ܕܡܢ ܠܛܒܬܐ ܐܝܬܝܗ̇ ܠܗܘܢ ܡܫܘܚܬܐ ܕܡܫܘܚܬܐ.

3) Compare, with this idea of the emanation of matter and evil from God, the same idea as expressed in the Zohar: this is one of the strongest coincidences which can be traced, and one of the clearest traces of

a confused sense of their place (?). *And I openly say, with entire frankness, that they were Tohu and Bohu* 1).

After innumerable ages had passed, the Good was moved to pour forth its love, and to brood over these unconscious minds, *in order that they should acquire the motion of life and consciousness; then there was born in them a new heart and a new spirit to know good and evil* 2): that is, it (the Good) endowed them with free-will, and then established the position of each essence according to the measure of its love. *It also made Christ head and ruler over them*, and *this took place when the mind received reason* 3). To some

---

Kabbalism in Hierotheos. According to the Zohar, the *En-Soph* or ancient of ancients, before it had put on a form, — before the manifestation of the Sephiroth, — produced formless worlds which were emitted from it like sparks. These could not subsist but *fell*, because the Adam Kadmon (as individualizing the 10 Sephiroth), which was to mediate between the creation and the *En-Soph*, had not yet been created. These worlds fell and were *little above nothing*, representing passive existence and the feminine principle, where all is resistance and inertia, as in matter (Tohu and Bohu). When the universal form of man (Adam Kadmon the mediator) was established, these ancient fallen worlds furnished the material element in the existing created universe (see Franck, *La Kabbale*, pp. 206, 207 and passim). This resistant passive principle is individualized in Hierotheos by the unredeemable and irrational *insensible essence* (see page 104).

1) ܒܪ ܒܬܪ ܠܟܠܗܘܢ ܐܟܚܕܐ ܒܪܫܬ ܡܦܠܘܬܐ ܕܡܛܝ ܠܬܚܬܝܬܐ. ܛܠܘܬܐ ܚܫܘܟܬܐ ܘܫܬܩܬܐ ܥܠ ܟܠܗܘܢ ܦܪܣ ܗܘܐ. ܕܦܫܢ ܕܝܢ ܠܡܕܡ ܕܠܐ ܐܝܬܘܗܝ: ܒܒܪ ܡܢ ܠܒܘܫܬܐ ܕܒܝܬܗܘܢ (?) ܡܒܝܢ. ܘܐܡܪ ܐܢܐ ܒܓܠܐ ܙܪ ܒܦܪܗܣܝܐ ܪܒܬܐ. ܕܬܘܗܘ ܘܒܘܗܘ ܐܝܬܝܗܘܢ ܗܘܘ.

2) ܕܢܩܢܘܢ ܙܘܥܐ ܕܚܝܐ ܘܕܝܕܥܬܐ: ܗܝܕܝܢ ܐܬܝܠܕ ܒܗܘܢ ܠܒܐ ܚܕܬܐ ܘܪܘܚܐ ܚܕܬܐ ܠܡܕܥ ܛܒܬܐ ܘܒܝܫܬܐ:

3) ܠܗ ܕܝܢ ܠܡܫܝܚܐ ܪܫܐ ܘܡܕܒܪܢܐ ܥܠ ܟܠܗܘܢ ܥܒܕܬ .... ܕܗܠܝܢ ܗܘ ܒܙܒܢܐ ܗܘ: ܕܗܘ ܩܒܠ ܗܘܢܐ ܡܠܬܐ.

minds, however, was left by the Good their unconscious and irrational essence (as the powers of evil), — but even they will eventually be redeemed. One essence, also, immediately on receiving consciousness began to oppose itself to the Good, and unto it were assigned the places under the earth.

The Universal Essence (from which all minds were directly separated) *is called universal, as it existed after separation from the Good, and before this ordered distinction: for to it came all that which was separated from the Good, and from it came forth every nature which appears separately and distinctly. For all minds were then confusedly mingled in it, without distinction and without consciousness; and, when they acquired the consciousness of distinction, they came forth from it* [1]. *Those however which remained within the limits of this essence acquired a superior consciousness; and to them does it pertain to reveal to divine minds, when they (the minds) reach them* [2], *the glorious and holy doctrines of the divine mysteries* [3].

---

1) The same idea seems to be expressed by Pseudo-Dionysios (Div. Names V, 5) when he says that God, »pre-possessing and super-posses»sing the anteriority and preëminence of being, caused the *universal* »*essence* (*τὸ εἶναι πᾶν*) to pre-exist; and from the universal essence itself »caused being, of whatever kind it be, to exist". Dionysios, by saying that the universal essence pre-existed, means that it came into being before all distinct and particular existence. Cf. Div. N. XI, 6. In this simple presentation of the same ideas is exhibited, better than by any comment, the radical difference between the thought of the seer Hierotheos and the philosopher Dionysios.

2) That is, during the ascent of the minds towards the Good.

3) L. I, ch. 8. ܕܟܠܝܐ ܕܝܢ ܐܬܦܪܫܬ: ܐܟܡܢ ܕܗܝ، ܐܬܝܬܗ ܒܬܪ ܦܘܠܓܐ ܕܡܢ ܛܒܬܐ: ܘܩܕܡ ܦܘܪܫܢܐ ܗܢܘ ܡܛܟܣܐ. ܠܗ ܓܝܪ ܐܬܬ ܟܠ ܕܡܢ ܛܒܬܐ ܐܬܦܪܫ. ܘܡܢܗ ܓܝܪ ܢܦܩ ܟܠ ܟܝܢܐ ܕܠܦܪܫܐܝܬ ܘܦܪܝܫܐܝܬ ܡܬܚܙܐ. ܟܕ ܕܝܢ ܗܘܘܢ ܕܠܐ ܦܘܪܫܢ ܘܕܠܐ ܡܕܥ: ܟܠܗܘܢ ܗܘܢܐ ܒܗ ܚܠܝܛܝܢ

As to the number of celestial essences, they are innumerable; but may be distinguished, as S. Paul says, into nine orders, each with three divisions, and again each of these containing nine distinctions. All have received different offices; some are sanctifiers, some helpers, some guides. Each one illuminates and influences the essence below it, but has no knowledge of the one above it.

BOOK SECOND.

What is the glory by which we must glorify [the Good], natural or supernatural? *To me it seems right to speak without words, and to understand without knowledge, that which is above words and knowledge: this I apprehend to be nothing but the mysterious silence and mystical quiet which destroys consciousness and dissolves forms. Seek therefore, silently and mystically, that perfect and primitive union with the essential Arch-Good* [1]).

ܗܘܘ: ܘܒܬܪ ܗܠܝܢ ܕܫܠܡܬܐ ܕܦܘܪܫܢܐ. ܡܢܘ ܠܢ ܐܡܪ ܠܗܘܢ
ܢܗܘ ܀ ܐܠܐ ܐܝܟ ܕܡܬܚܫܒܐ ܕܐܘܣܝܐ ܗܝ، ܐܬܒܥܘ.
ܕܒܗ ܬܫܒܘܚܬܐ ܡܢܗ. ܐܦ ܠܢ ܕܠܗܘܢ ܗܘ، ܠܟܠܗ
ܠܗܘܢܐ ܐܠܗܝܐ. ܡܟܐ ܕܠܬܚܬܗܘܢ ܡܬܬܟܠܝܢ. ܘܐܬܝܕܥܘܗ
ܫܠܝܐ ܘܡܫܬܩܢܘܬܐ ܕܐܝܬܝܐ ܐܠܗܝܐ.

1) ܠܐ ܡܢ ܡܫܬܡܥܢܐ ܕܗܘ ܕܒܠܐ ܡܠܬܐ ܠܡܡܠܠܘ: ܘܕܠܐ
ܡܕܥܐ ܠܡܕܥ. ܗܘ ܡܐ ܕܠܥܠ ܡܢ ܡܠܬܐ ܘܡܕܥܐ. ܠܐ
ܐܚܪܢܐ ܕܐܝܬܘܗܝ ܐܠܐ ܫܬܩܐ ܚܫܝܐ ܘܫܠܝܐ ܕܐܪ̈ܐܙܐ. ܕܡܒܛܠ
ܪ̈ܓܫܐ ܘܡܫܪܐ ܐܣܟܡ̈ܐ. ܒܥܘ ܕܝܢ ܫܬܝܩܐܝܬ ܘܐܪܙܢܝܐܝܬ:
ܠܚܝܕܝܘܬܐ ܗܝ، ܓܡܝܪܬܐ ܘܪܫܝܬܐ ܕܥܡ ܪܫ ܛܒܘܬܐ
ܐܝܬܝܬܐ.

Motion and purification are the acts by which we glorify the Arch-Good. The first motion, as has been said, was a descendent one, out of Nature [1]: but there are many motions, some ascendent, and others descendent.

Natural motion belongs to the fully developed condition of those who have not yet received the meat of knowledge but are still fed on milk. *Post-natural motion* is found in those who (while in a natural condition) *desire to live in an ordered manner*, and comprises *many divisions, like the angelic and super-angelic. Extra-natural motion* appertains to those who have a tendency towards evil in the natural sphere, and are then called sinners, and afterwards beasts and animals. *Super-natural motion* is that which is above the post-natural: instead of having many divisions and degrees and being governed by forms (as the latter is), it is *a still and silent perturbation, a proceeding without a way, and a knowledge raised above forms*; still it desires because it is not confusedly mingled. *Ultra-natural motion* is beyond the extra-natural, for it belongs to demons and to those minds which have completely left the whole nature of the Good and acquired a certain union with the Prince (of Darkness) [2].

There exist in the space between earth and heaven three

1) For the explanation of this we must call attention to the absolute identification in Hierotheos of *nature* (ܟܝܢܐ), i. e. universal nature, with the arch-good (ܪܝܫܘܬ ܛܒܘܬܐ) or agatharchy (ἀγαθαρχία), the first principle, which in the beginning contained all things undistinguished within itself.

2) Of these six motions, three are vital and three destructive: the former are, in order of progression, the *natural, post-natural*, and *super-natural* (compare with the κόσμιος, περικόσμιος and ὑπερκόσμιος of Dionysios); the latter are, the original motion out of the Good, the *extra-natural* and the *ultra-natural*.

essences of demons, each of which has received its place according to the measure of its departure from the Good. The lower is darker than the upper, and wages a fiercer war against minds during their ascendent motion. While the mind possesses natural motion, it is combated by the first of these essences; when post-natural, by the two lower: and when it ascends (supernaturally), it is overwhelmed by all of them, for they desire to make it like unto themselves.

Ascent of the mind.

Now the end of the labor of minds is this glorious ascent, for God does not desire that minds should fall, and wishes to bring them back unto himself. Those who desire to rise (unto the Father) must unite the Good-Nature which is in them with its essence, and remove from themselves all traces of the opposing principle. To do this, they must purify their soul and body, that their garments may be clean; otherwise they will fall in the ascent. When the mind ascends, the body is as if dead, and the soul is absorbed in the mind, which is carried up and becomes oblivious of everything on earth. All the essences of demons gather together to oppose it; but it vanquishes them, and the Lord raises it with the hand of his goodness up to the firmament, and the angelic hosts cry out: *Lift up your heads, O ye gates, and the king of glory shall enter* [1]).

When the mind is made worthy to ascend above the firmament, which is the middle wall of separation, *it is like*

---

1) Psalm XXIV, 7.

a new-born child which passes from darkness unto light. During the labor of its ascent the mind is strengthened by its own natural desire for absorption, and by the aid it receives from the various essences through which it passes, and which communicate successively unto it the mysteries of their knowledge. As the mind rises, it becomes the purifier and sanctifier of the essences below it, and partakes, with those through which it passes, of the sacrament of the Eucharist, by which it communicates unto them the perfection of its intelligence and receives from them the mysteries of their order. These essences, recognizing in it the supreme nature of the Good, assemble also to offer it adoration. Having passed the multitude of heavens, the mind arrives in the place called *distinction*, which is the boundary separating the upper world from our own: here does it rest from its labors. Then proceeding on its way, it reaches the holy place of the Cross: here it understands that it is to endure its passion and suffer crucifixion, in the same manner that Christ suffered; for unless the mind undergoes all that Christ suffered, it cannot be perfected. Then is the mind crucified in the centre by the angels, who, from being its worshippers, are turned into its haters: while the soul and body, being separated from it, are crucified, the former on its right and the latter on its left. Then is sin vanquished and destroyed. This is to be understood figuratively and symbolically.

The sufferings of the cross may have to be endured more than once, nay ten or even twenty times; as many as there are grades separating the mind from the primary essence. *For all minds do not descend into bodies from one essence alone*, but from many [1]): these essences are more or less

1) This is strongly Origenistic.

perfect according to their descent from the Good. Thus those minds which descended from the essence of the Father need but one purification by the cross; those which descended from that of the Son need two, and from the Holy Spirit three; and thus through the entire legion of essences. ***Minds come into the body also from the essence of demons.***

When all is consummated, the mind is laid in the sepulchre to rest there for three days.

BOOK THIRD.

On the third day the mind rises and reunites unto itself its purified soul and body, which in this new, unchangeable, and immortal life are subjected unto it, having been in the former life its subjectors. Although by this experience the mind has become greatly purified, yet, as its sins have been many, it must undergo many purifications. The Good-principle in it has a still greater desire to unite itself unto its essence, and by it becomes transfigured before the eyes of the angels. Now does it acquire the motion of union [1]. Nevertheless the root of evil and opposition has not yet been eradicated from it, but, gathering its forces, begins to re-appear, and grows up into an immense tree, whose wide-spreading branches cast darkness over divine minds and shade them from the perfect light of the Good. In the long and terrible combat which follows, the mind many times cuts down and destroys the branches of the tree, but it ever shoots anew with equal strength from the undestroyed root. Finally by

---

1) That is of identification with Christ.

divine illumination the mind sees that it must descend to the lowest regions, where the roots of the tree of evil are planted, and eradicate them. Then begins for the mind a sorrowful return, through the regions by which it had ascended, down below the earth. There it combats with the fierce demons of the North, South, East and West, and, finally, is vanquished and slain by them. Immediately however Christ, the great mind, is revealed, opens the gates of Sche'ol, and descending brings to life and raises up the mind from the infernal regions. It again swiftly and peacefully makes its second ascent through the regions which it formerly traversed. It is then made worthy of the spiritual baptism of the Spirit and of fire, without which there is no life. After this there is no obstacle to the mind being in everything not merely like unto but identical with Christ, and it receives the adoration of all the heavenly hosts, for it now obtains the power of divine high-priesthood, and is made worthy of union with the Good. The mind is now no longer mind, but is the Son, who doeth all according to his will, is judge of all, creates and makes alive, orders and constitutes. Christ is no longer adored, but minds, *for Christ is nothing but the mind purified, which can say: all power is given unto me in Heaven and in earth* [1]), *and, there is no God beside me* [2]). *For Christ is the Lord of those who are asleep, and not of those who are awakened* [3]).

---

1) Matthew XXVIII, 18. 2) Isaiah XLV, 5 etc.

3) ܠܐ ܡܪܐ ܐܝܬܘܗܝ ܡܫܝܚܐ. ܐܠܐ ܗܘܢܐ ܕܡܬܕܟܐ ܗܘ ܕܝܢ ܕܡܛܐ ܠܡܐܡܪ: ܕܐܬܝܗܒ ܠܝ ܟܠ ܫܘܠܛܢ ܕܒܫܡܝܐ ܘܒܐܪܥܐ... ܘܕܠܝܬ ܐܠܗܐ ܐܚܪܝܢ ܠܒܪ ܡܢܝ .... ܐܠܝܢ ܕܠܡܕܟܝܘܬܐ ܡܛܝܘܢ. ܘܡܫܡܠܝܢ ܠܝܬ ܠܗܘܢ ܡܫܝܚܐ ܪܥܝܐ. ܡܛܠ ܕܡܫܝܚܐ ܕܕܡܟܐ ܐܝܬܘܗܝ ܪܥܝܐ.

Then the mind, which is now Christ, communicates unto the angelic hosts, in the holy of holies, the spiritual Eucharist, of which the terrestrial is but the type and faint shadow. After this it rises again unto the place where there is no longer vision, to be united unto the tree of life, unto the Universal Essence.

BOOK FOURTH.

The Universal Essence has been previously defined, but only partially; in its essence, not in its operations. It is contemplated by the mind in mystery and silence, and the latter receives from it complete *love* and *union.* It also imparts unto the mind three mysterious and unspeakable doctrines:

that of the distinction of minds;
that of the coming of the mind into the body; and
what becomes of the nature of all things.

In all this is the mind instructed by the High-Priest of the Universal Essence, who lays upon it the solemn injunction of silence. Leaving him, the mind continues its ascent accompanied by all the essences perfected and sanctified by it. For all minds which are perfected must pass through all the stations and receive all the forms which are below the Good, and through which they had fallen. The mind has now reached Paradise, where *Adam by the first distinction suffered the fall*, and it is shown by the watch the way to the Tree of Life, unto which it desires to unite itself, for this would be *the consummation of visions and the perfection of mysteries.* But now the Adversary, Satan, knowing its desire, changes himself into the semblance of the Tree of Life, and is revealed as *the Man of Sin, the Son of Perdition, sitting as God in the temple of God* [1]) *and saying: I am the bread which came down from heaven; whoso eateth of me shall live for ever* [2]). The mind therefore, being deceived, hastens to unite itself unto this evil essence, which appears unto it as the Tree of Life. Then is Christ, the great mind, revealed, to take vengeance on this deceptive nature: he stamps it to the ground and burns it with fire, having separated from it the Good-nature of the mind. Finally the mind, led by Christ, approaches unto and unites itself with the Tree of Life and possesses quiet and rest. Men say that the Tree of Life is Christ, but I say that it is above him.

When the mind desires to pass this place, it is told: *remain in thy place.* It then receives a mystic sword, with which to exterminate the demons, the enemies of the Lord, by descending to the places under the earth: *for the Father judgeth no man, but has committed all judgment unto the Son* [3]). It again takes a downward course, and this time with joy, for it knows that the adversative nature cannot, as at first, oppose it. The divine mind enters the gates of She'ol, and all the essences of demons gather themselves

---

1) II Thessal. II, 3.

2) John VI, 51. The Syriac text reads: ܒܪܢܫܐ ܕܚܛܝܬܐ ܒܪܗ ܕܐܒܕܢܐ - ܘܒܗܝܟܠܐ ܕܐܠܗܐ (ܕܐܬܘܗܝ، ܐܬܝܒ ܗܘ ܥܕܒܝܫܐ.) ܐܝܟ ܐܠܗܐ ܢܬܒ. ܘܢܐܡܪ ܥܠ ܢܦܫܗ ܕܐܢܐ ܐܢܐ. ܗܘ ܠܗܬ، ܐܢܐ ܐܢܐ ܠܚܡܐ ܕܡܢ ܫܡܝܐ ܢܚܬܬ ܀ .. ܡܢ ܟܢ ܕܠ ܢܐܟܘܠ ܢܐܚܐ ܠܥܠܡ.

3) John V, 22.

together to combat against it; but they are overthrown and destroyed, and the minds suffering torments are delivered, enlightened and forgiven. The infernal regions also are illuminated and purified, so that they are no whit less bright than the celestial regions. Now has the mind cast out from itself the whole of the adversative nature: it wishes also to destroy the head of opposition, and sees that it is what had appeared to it as the Tree of Life, and so cuts it down. All the minds which had been slaves to perdition now desire to be united to the Divine Mind and saved; but, as is meet for the Son, it orders judgment and adjudges torments to sinners and demons, and descends further to the place of the Prince of darkness, and finally to the Sun and the Moon: this infernal sun is a gift of the Good, in order that the rational beings in this place should not perish. When the mind has passed She'ol and the lowest abyss, it reaches the place where there is no longer vision. Still lower, in the place below all places, are the roots of evil, which it is moved to destroy. Now when it is said that the mind destroys demons, it is meant that *it destroys them in itself and not in their essence;* and when it destroys these roots, it means that *it will be united unto the Good alone.*

After the mind has thus decreed judgment in Gehenna, it desires to see the *Insensible Essence*, which is the rebellious essence. This does not possess any name that is named on the earth or under the earth, neither does it possess anything of nature [1]: those who are imprisoned in it cannot obtain resurrection or life. It is irrational, unconscious, lifeless, and insensible, and has received the name of *Not-being.* In the beginning it bore no fruits, and, after being proved,

---

1) i. e. of the Good: cf. p. 97 n. 1.

it was condemned and fell from being mind, first to being man, then animal, beast, demon, devil, and finally became insensible and contumacious, having entirely left its Good and its Nature. Although the mind stretches out its hand unto it, yet does it not submit.

All is now fulfilled in the places under the earth: the mind, as it begins its ascent, sees all those whom it has slain lying before it, and is moved with great desire to become the Father, to raise them all from the dead, and to have mercy upon them. Then will it extend its goodness unto all, both good and evil, *and make them all like itself.* Then there comes a wonderful voice before the resurrection crying: *Come from the four winds, O breath, and breathe upon these slain that they may live* [1]). All the minds which descended from Essence are raised and approach the Divine Mind, which says unto them: *Ye are my brethren: for truly are ye bone of my bones, and flesh of my flesh* [2]); and they are united unto it in order that they may ascend with it.

When the Divine Mind has passed all this, it descends below all essences and sees a luminous essence whose divine light is *formless*: it marvels greatly that this is the same essence which it had seen on high. Now does it comprehend the true theory of Essence, — that it fills the whole universe, — and cries: *If I ascend up into heaven, thou art there, and if I descend to hell, there also art thou. And if I raise the wings of my understanding like those of the eagle, and dwell in the uttermost parts of the sea, even there shall thy hand lead me, and thy right hand shall hold me* [3]).

---

1) Ezechiel XXXVII, 9.
2) Genesis II, 23.
3) Psalm CXXXIX, 8—10.

The mind approaches and unites itself unto this luminous essence, and looks above and below, the length and the breadth, and encloses in itself everything. It will now no longer ascend or descend, for it is all-containing [1]).

The mind has now left the name of Christ, for it has passed distinction, reason, and word, and it will no longer be said: *Father glorify thy Son that thy Son also may glorify thee* [2]), for all distinction of the glorifier and the glorified has passed away. Love also (the Spirit) is still a sign of distinction, for it implies a person loving and one loved; — this also do perfect minds pass beyond, for they go beyond every name that is named.

For when distinction [3]) *arose, all perfect and holy minds*

---

1) This is the *Ultima Thule* of Pantheistic absorption. What follows is not posterior in time, but simply contemplates the same result from a different standpoint.

2) John XVII, 1.

3) We give as a specimen the entire 21st chapter of the fourth book, entitled ܥܠ ܚܘܒܐ »On love", from which the passage here quoted is taken. ܥܠ ܚܘܒܐ ܘܕܡܢܐ ܐܝܬܘܬܗ، ܚܘܒܐ ܘܕܐܠܥܠܡ ܬܘܒ ܚܕܝܢ؛ ܐܝܟ ܡܫܘܚܐ ܐܝܟ. ܐܝܬܘܬܗ، ܠܘܬ ܚܘܒܐ ܫܘܡܠܝܘܬܐ ܕܚܕܝܘܬܐ ܘܡܙܝܓܘܬܐ. ܕܐܣܦܝܪܐ ܐܠܗܝܬܐ ܘܢܘܗܪܐ ܬܡܗܝܢܘܬ. ܠܗܘ ܡܢܐ ܕܠܫܝܢܘܬܐ ܡܫܒܚ. ܐܝܟ ܕܝܢ ܠܥܠܡ ܕܗܘܝܐ ܚܕ ܐܝܟ. ܕܕܘܟܝܢ ܠܟ ܐܦ ܡܢ ܚܕܝܘܬܐ. ܗܟܐ ܠܒܪ ܘܟܠܗ ܕܚܘܒܐ ܐܬܐ ܐܝܬܘܬܗ، ܕܦܘܪܫܢܐ. ܠܐ ܠܒܪ ܡܬܚܫܒ ܚܘܒܐ ܡܢ ܚܕ. ܐܠܐ ܡܢ ܬܪܝܢ. ܡܢ ܡܫܒܚܢܐ ܘܡܢ ܗܘ ܕܠܗ ܡܫܒܚ. ܡܕܡ ܡܢ ܡܠܬ ܕܦܘܪܫܢܐ ܡܕܡ ܬܪܝܢܐ ܐܝܬܘܗܝ، ܫܡܗܐ ܗܢܐ ܕܚܘܒܐ. ܐܝܟܢ ܐܬܚܘܒܬ ܡܢܝ ܒܡܫܠܡܢܘܬܐ ܬܪܝܨܬܐ. ܕܐܦ ܗܘ ܚܘܒܐ ܐܝܬܝܗ ܗܘ

were both glorified and glorifiers: glorified by men and an-

ܕܦܘܪܩܢܐ. ܚܙܐ ܕܝܢ ܘܠܫܘܒܚܐ ܐܝܟ ܕܡܫܒܚܝܢ. ܕܐܝܢܐ
ܥܒܕܐ ܠܗܘܢ ܙܕܩ ܘܐܡܬܝ ܕܠܒܐ ܡܢ ܥܒܕܐ ܗܘ ܕܝܕܝܥܘܬܐ
ܢܬܬܚܒܪ ܠܝ ܕܐܝܬܘܗܝ، ܒܗܢܘܢ ܡܫܒܚܢܐ ܕܫܘܒܚܐ. ܐܢܬ ܕܝܢ
ܒܪ، ܠܐ ܒܠܚܘܕ ܝܚܝܕ ܫܘܒܚܐ ܬܗܘܐ. ܐܠܐ ܘܠܪܘܚܡܬܐ
ܥܒܕܬ. ܘܠܚܕܘܬܐ ܚܒܪ. ܕܬܬܬܚܒܪ ܕܝܢ ܒܪܐܝܐ ܥܒܝܕܐ
ܠܟܠ ܡܢ ܫܘܒܚܐ ܘܪܘܚܡܬܐ ܘܚܕܘܬܐ ܠܡܗܘܐ. ܐܢܐ ܕܝܢ ܒܪ،
ܘܠܐ ܠܗܕܐ ܕܡܬܩܪܐ ܪܘܚܡܬܐ ܡܫܒܚ ܐܢܐ. ܐܦ ܒܗ̇
ܡܕܡ ܕܦܘܪܩܢܐ ܚܙܐ ܐܢܐ. ܐܠܘ ܓܝܪ ܠܐܢܫܐ ܕܪܚܡ
ܕܠܐܢܫܐ ܢܗܘܐ ܪܚܡ. ܘܡܢ ܡܛܠ ܕܝܢ ܘܠܐܢܫܐ ܕܡܬܪܚܡ.
ܡܢ ܡܕܡ ܐܚܪܢܐ ܐܦ ܗ̇ܘ ܡܬܪܚܡ. ܡܕܝܢ ܠܐ ܡܟܝܠ
ܪܚܡܝܢ ܐܢܘ ܡܚܒܝܢ. ܗܟܢܐ ܐܝܟ ܕܠܡܬܪܚܡܘܬܐ ܐܬܩܢܘ.
ܢܦܫܢ ܓܝܪ ܠܒܐ ܡܢܗܘܢ ܟܠ ܥܒܕܐ ܕܡܬܩܪܐ ܘܦܪܘܫ
ܘܡܫܘܐ ܡܕܡ. ܘܗܘܝܢ ܡܟܝܠ ܕܠܐ ܥܒܕܐ ܠܟܠ ܡܢ ܥܒܕܐ.
ܘܕܠܐ ܡܠܬܐ ܠܟܠ ܡܢ ܡܠܬܐ. ܗܐ ܓܝܪ ܘܥܒܕܐ ܕܡܫܒܚܐ
ܐܬܐ ܡܕܡ ܐܝܬܘܗܝ، ܠܝ. ܕܗ̇ܘ ܡܢܐ ܕܡܫܒܚ. ܘܕܐܝܢܐ
ܕܡܫܬܒܚ. ܡܢ ܡܛܠ ܓܝܪ ܡܫܒܚܢܐ ܘܡܫܬܒܚܢܐ. ܠܐ
ܗܘܐ ܚܕ ܐܠܐ ܬܪܝܢ. ܐܢܕܝܢ ܐܢܬ ܐܡܪܬ، ܕܠܐ ܢܬܡܪܐ
ܗܘܢܐ ܬܪܝܢ ܒܗܢ ܠܒܐ: ܐܝܟܢܐ ܗ̇، ܠܝ ܐܦ ܫܒܩܐ
ܕܡܫܒܚܐ ܠܡܫܒܚܘ. ܐܝܟܢܐ ܓܝܪ ܕܐܒܐ ܕܒܪܐ ܐܝܬܘܗܝ،
ܐܒܐ: ܘܒܪܐ ܬܘܒ ܕܐܒܐ ܐܝܬܘܗܝ، ܒܪܐ. ܬܪܝܢ ܡܕܝܢ
ܐܝܬܝܗܘܢ ܡܢ ܡܛܠ. ܐܒܐ ܘܗ̇ܘ ܕܒܪܐ ܡܫܬܡܗܝܢ. ܐܢܐ
ܕܝܢ ܠܗܘܢܐ ܓܡܝܪܐ ܚܙܐ ܐܢܐ. ܕܠܐ ܡܟܝܠ ܦܪܘܫ:
ܘܐܝܢܐ ܕܦܪܘܫ ܐܒܐ ܒܪܐ ܐܝܬܘܗܝ، ܥܒܕ ܕܝܢ ܡܕܝܢ
ܗܘܢܐ ܫܘܒܚܐ ܕܒܪܘܬܐ. ܐܡܬܝ، ܕܕܠܐ ܦܘܪܩܢܐ ܢܬܒܥ.

gels and by the superior and inferior essences, and glorifying the Good alone which was above them. Now when distinction is removed, they are glorified and are no longer glorifiers; for whom should they glorify, as the Good is in them and they in it? granting it correct to use the expressions in it *and* in them, *for one is the nature and one the person of them and of it; granting it correct to use the terms* of them *and* of it. *Neither will they any longer be named heirs, for distinction is blotted out from them, and when there is no distinction, who can inherit from another? Come now, therefore, and let us glorify with unutterable glory the mind which no longer glorifies but is glorified.*

Neither does the mind receive permanently the name of

ܠܐ ܓܝܪ ܐܬܘܗܝ ܡܬܦܪܫܢܐ: ܡܢ ܩܕܝܡ ܓܝܪ ܢܬܦܪܫ.
ܕܗܘܐ ܠܐ ܦܠܛ ܡܢ ܦܘܫܕܐ. ܒܬܪܟܢ ܓܝܪ ܕܗܘܐ ܦܘܪܫܢܐ.
ܡܫܒܚܢܐ ܓܝܪ ܘܡܫܬܒܚܢܐ ܐܬܝܗܘܢ ܗܘ̈ܢܐ ܟܠܗܘܢ
ܒܡܬ̈ܪܐ ܘܩܕ̈ܝܫܐ. ܡܫܬܒܚܝܢ ܓܝܪ ܡܢ ܐܝ̈ܢܐ ܘܡܢ ܡ̈ܠܐܟܐ
ܘܡܢ ܐܘܣ̈ܝܐ ܕܠܥܠ ܘܕܠܬܚܬ. ܡܫܒܚܝܢ ܕܝܢ ܗܘܘ ܠܛܒܐ
ܒܠܚܘܕ ܕܠܥܠ ܡܢܗܘܢ. ܡܐ ܕܝܢ ܕܐܬܬܥܝܪ ܦܘܪܫܢܐ.
ܡܫܬܒܚܢܐ ܐܬܝܗܘܢ ܘܠܐ ܡܫܒ̈ܚܢܐ. ܠܡܢܘ ܓܝܪ
ܢܫܒܚܘܢ. ܕܗܘܐ ܛܒܐ ܒܗܘܢ ܘܗܢܘܢ ܒܗ. ܐܢ ܙܕܩ ܗ̇ܝ
ܕܒܗ ܘܒܗܘܢ ܠܡܐܡܪ. ܕܚܕ ܗ̣ܘ ܓܝܪ ܚܕ ܟܝܢܐ
ܘܚܕ ܩܢܘܡܐ ܕܝܠܗܘܢ ܘܕܝܠܗ. ܐܢ ܙܕܩ ܕܕܝܠܗܘܢ ܘܕܝܠܗ
ܠܡܐܡܪ. ܘܠܐ ܕܝܢ ܬܘܒ ܝܪ̈ܬܐ ܢܬܩܪܘܢ. ܡܛܠ ܕܐܬܥܛܝ
ܠܗ ܡܢܗܘܢ ܦܘܪܫܢܐ. ܟܕ ܕܝܢ ܕܠܝܬ ܦܘܪܫܢܐ: ܡܢܘ ܠܡܢܘ
ܢܪܬ. ܬܐ ܡܕܝܢ ܒܫܘܒܚܐ ܕܠܐ ܡܬܡܠܠ ܢܫܒܚܘܗܝ. ܠܗܘܢܐ
ܗܘ ܕܠܐ ܡܫܒܚ ܬܘܒ ܐܠܐ ܡܫܬܒܚ ܀

Divinity; for this implies mercy and desire. To describe what the mind undergoes during this process is beyond the power of words.

It will then begin[1]*, by a new and holy brooding, to create a new world, and will create a new man in its image imageless, and according to its likeness likenessless. It will mete out heaven with its span, and will measure the dust of the earth with its measure: it will number the drops of the sea, and weigh the mountains in a scale*[2]*. And who will speak of it, that cannot be spoken? or name it, that cannot be named? Let us, with the apostle, marvel at a mystery and say: "Oh the depth and the riches, the wisdom and understanding, above the name of divinity, of the perfect mind when perfected. For man cannot comprehend its judgments, and its ways are inscrutable*[3]*. For who hath known its mind? or who hath been its counsellor?*[4]

---

1) ܘܡܫܪܐ ܢܒܪܐ ܒܪܘܚܦܘܬܐ ܚܕܬܐ ܘܩܕܝܫܬܐ ܥܠܡܐ ܚܕܬܐ
ܠܡܒܪܐ. ܘܢܒܪܐ ܒܪܢܫܐ ܚܕܬܐ ܒܨܠܡܗ ܕܠܐ ܨܠܡܐ:
ܘܒܕܡܘܬܗ ܕܠܐ ܕܡܘܬܐ. ܘܢܡܫܘܚ ܫܡܝܐ ܒܙܪܬܗ. ܘܢܟܝܠ
ܒܟܝܠܗ ܥܦܪܗ ܕܐܪܥܐ. ܘܢܡܢܐ ܢܛܦ̈ܬܐ ܕܝܡܐ. ܘܢܬܩܘܠ
ܛܘܪ̈ܐ ܒܡܬܩܠܐ. ܘܡܢܘ ܡܡܠܠ ܠܐܡܬܡܪܢܘܬܗ ܕܠܐ ܡܬܐܡܪ.
ܘܡܢܘ ܢܫܡܝܘܗܝ ܕܠܐ ܡܬܫܡܗ. ܒܪܡ ܕܝܢ ܢܬܕܡܪ ܒܪܐܙܐ
ܥܡ ܫܠܝܚܐ ܘܢܐܡܪ. ܐܘ̄ ܥܘܡܩܐ ܘܥܘܬܪܐ ܘܚܟܡܬܐ
ܘܣܘܟܠܐ. ܕܠܥܠ ܡܢ ܫܡܗܐ ܕܐܠܗܘܬܐ. ܕܗܘܢܐ ܓܡܝܪܐ
ܕܐܫܬܡܠܝ. ܐܝܟ ܓܒܪ ܠܐ ܡܫ ܕܢܕܥܝܘܗܝ. ܘܐܘܪܚܬܗ ܠܐ
ܡܬܒܨܝܢ. ܡܢܘ ܓܝܪ ܝ̈ܕܥ ܪܥܝܢܗ. ܐܘ ܡܢܘ ܗܘܐ ܠܗ
ܒܥܠ ܡܠܟܐ:

2) Isaiah XL, 12.
3) Romans XI, 33—34.
4) Isaiah XL, 14.

This is but a small part of the glories of the Mind when it accomplishes all and is confusedly mingled with the Good, the universal Creator.

We must now point out the distinction between union[1]) and absorption[2]), and show whether Christ be united or absorbed. In *Union* that which is distinguished does not appear very distinct: but those things which are united cannot throw off all distinction, for in them exists the principle which distinguishes. On the contrary, in those things which are *absorbed* nothing appears which distinguishes or makes other. Therefore to Christ we give the name of *our union.* To absorption can no name be given.

BOOK FIFTH.

All these doctrines, which are unknown even to angels, have I disclosed unto thee, my son, even though I be, on this account, despised of men. Know then, that *all nature will be confused* with the Father: that nothing will perish or be destroyed, but all will return, be sanctified, united and confused. Thus God will be all in all. Even hell will pass away and the damned return. All orders and distinctions will cease. God will pass away, and Christ will cease to

---

1) ܚܕܝܘܬܐ.

2) ܚܒܝܟܘܬܐ: the only definition in Payne-Smith is *commixtio*, but the cognates ܚܘܒܟܢܐ and ܚܘܒܟܐ are rendered by *confusio.* The two meanings seem inseparable from the root: therefore I have rendered the verb always by *confusedly mingled*: in the noun it seemed more expressive, as well as rendering more completely the author's meaning, to use the term *absorption.*

be, and the Spirit will no longer be called spirit. Essence alone will remain.

In the same way that all rational nature is governed by its laws, so also all irrational nature obeys its special laws.

»My son, preserve my words, place them around thy neck, and let them be a sign on thy forehead", for the time has come that I should pass away: unto thee do I bequeath the sceptre of my right hand.

www.ingramcontent.com/pod-product-compliance
Lightning Source LLC
Chambersburg PA
CBHW070632220426
R18178600001B/R181786PG43193CBX00019B/27
* 9 7 8 1 6 0 8 9 9 6 0 7 0 *